"When we founded rabble.ca 20 years ago, Canada urgently needed an online centre of gravity for radical news. This urgency feels even greater today. I'm so happy rabble is still going strong."

MARK SURMAN, executive director, Mozilla Foundation, and rabble.ca co-founder

"Rabble.ca's greatest strengths have always been its digital-first birthright and its singular passion for—as mainstream media once trumpeted but no longer triumphs—afflicting the comfortable and comforting the afflicted. The act of affliction often requires diverse voices acting in concert, being amplified by the timely megaphone of a sympathetic medium and by compassionate craftspeople. You'll find all of that here. Consider this book a thorn in the side of complacency."

WAYNE MACPHAIL, former director of Southam InfoLab and founder of the rabble.ca podcast network

"At a time when many cash-strapped newsrooms struggle to cover even basic news, we need more local rabbles to champion other ways of seeing the world, suggest alternatives, and challenge prevailing wisdoms."

APRIL LINDGREN, Professor and Velma Rogers Research Chair, Ryerson School of Journalism

"The book is a remarkably rich collection of some of the best of rabble.ca's thousands of articles published over its twenty-year history, and contemporary essays on their continued relevance. Covering key topic themes over the years, the combination of analysis with stories based on personal experience illustrates some of the best independent, movement- and justice-oriented journalism that Canada has to offer. A highly readable, engaging and valuable resource for students and teachers of alternative media, journalism, and politics, that will also attract readers interested in Canadian politics and social justice."

ROBERT HACKETT, Professor Emeritus of communication, Simon Fraser University

Everything on (the) Line

Everything on (the) Line

20 years of social movement stories from rabble.ca

edited by Sophia Reuss
and Christina Turner

Between the Lines
Toronto

Everything on (the) Line

First published in 2021 by
Between the Lines
401 Richmond Street West, Studio 281
Toronto, Ontario · M5V 3A8 · Canada
1-800-718-7201 · www.btlbooks.com

Cataloguing in Publication information available from
Library and Archives Canada · ISBN 9781771135443

Cover and text design by DEEVE

Printed in Canada

We acknowledge for their financial support of our publishing activities: the Government of Canada; the Canada Council for the Arts; and the Government of Ontario through the Ontario Arts Council, the Ontario Book Publishers Tax Credit program, and Ontario Creates.

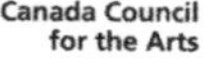

Conseil des Arts du Canada

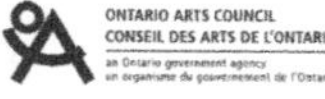

Contents

Acknowledgements

The idea for this book predates our time as rabble.ca staff. Thank you to Maya Bhullar, Jessica Rose, and Kim Elliott, whose early work on a rabble.ca anthology guided our ideas and vision. Thank you to former editors for your work on the early best of rabble anthologies, which were invaluable as we dove into the site's massive archive.

Thank you to Kim Elliott for trusting two rookie book editors with a big idea and a twenty-year-old archive. Thank you to Matthew Adams, Matthew DiMera, Jessica Rose, and Phillip Dwight Morgan for shepherding this project and believing in us. Thanks to Tania Ehret for your patience and energy tracking down permissions. Thanks to Mark Surman and Judy Rebick for their insight into rabble's beginnings, the early internet, and independent media. Paige Sisley provided crucial advice about book proposals in this project's early stages, and Barbara Pulling was a source of perceptive feedback and generous support on the draft manuscript.

A huge debt of gratitude is owed to our partners, Matt Goerzen and Grant Hurley, for their vital support of our work, and for enduring endless Zoom calls conducted during the quarantine. Thank you to Treme Manning-Cere, Allison Smith, Emily Parr, Caroline Grego, Alana Boileau, and Jessica Rose for your friendship and ideas.

Thank you to our dozens of contributors, who took to rabble over the past twenty years to share their ideas and perspectives, and who allowed us to reprint their work in this book. Thank you to Monia Mazigh, Barâa Arar, Russell Diabo, Michael Stewart, Nora Loreto, Phillip Dwight Morgan, Kim Elliott, and Matthew Adams for your excellent analysis of social movement stories and Canadian history—and for your patience through several rounds of editing as we turned this idea into a book. *Everything on (the) Line* would not exist without the support of Amanda Crocker and Between the Lines, a fierce indie press that we are incredibly honoured to have worked with on this book.

Lastly, thank you to the activists, organizers, and ordinary people working to change our world for the better, one protest at a time. This book is for you.

Introduction

Sophia Reuss and
Christina Turner

As we write, a deadly pandemic has shut down Canada and much of the world. Borders are closed. Political leaders are weighing human life against economic growth as we hurtle towards a massive recession. Hundreds of thousands of people worldwide have died in just a few months, and many more have lost their jobs and livelihoods. There is no understating the impact: it is crushing, and this is just the beginning.

At the same time, the police murder of George Floyd, a Black man in America, has sparked mass protests around the world, shifting the needle on public discourse about police and prison abolition overnight. In the weeks since, recent police killings of Black and Indigenous people of colour in Canada—Regis Korchinsky-Paquet, D'Andre Campbell, Chantel Moore, Rodney Levi, Ejaz Ahmed Choudry—have forced a long overdue national conversation about state violence and racism. However these stories unfold, two things will remain true: the death and destruction that the coronavirus has wrought began with seeds planted long before the virus began to spread in Canada, and it is no coincidence that a global movement for racial justice ignited during a pandemic has thrown everyday realities of inequality and injustice into sharp relief. These are stories about racial capitalism, austerity, and a profit-driven economy hell-bent on extracting wealth from people and our planet.

There are traces of our current moment in an earlier one that unfolded twenty years ago. On April 21, 2001, some seventy-five thousand people flooded the streets of Quebec City to protest corporate globalization and a neoliberal trade deal. Over two days, thirty-four world leaders, including then Prime Minister Jean Chrétien and US President George W. Bush, gathered to discuss the Free Trade Area of the Americas. Outside the summit, demonstrators gathered around a three-metre-high barricade surrounded by police. Protesters organized themselves into three zones: a green zone, far away from the police lines, where protesters danced to music and walked in parades; a yellow zone, closer to the action; and a red zone, where militant protesters faced off with the police. At one point, a group of Black Bloc anarchists broke through a section of the security fence. These clashes were protracted and violent: police fired water cannons, bean bags, rubber bullets, and thousands of cans of tear gas directly into the crowd.

From the ground in Quebec City, stories about the protests populated a website launched just days before: rabble.ca. In the days that followed, rabble, a new independent media source run by a group of journalists and activists, would go on to publish dozens of stories about the Quebec City mobilizations. One Quebec City resident published a series of stories documenting daily life "behind the fence" in the St. Roch neighbourhood. She wrote about the atmosphere leading up to the Summit, as small businesses boarded up windows and the fence barricade was plastered with signs and information: "People stand along the fence reading. One sign says somewhat testily, 'Things on this fence have been put here to be helpful to people. Please don't steal them.' There are maps, balloons, t-shirts, banners, bras, pieces of cardboard, paintings, information sheets, tapestries, quilts. The fence is becoming beautiful."

Elsewhere on the site, Ali Kazimi, a filmmaker documenting a group of students at the protests, wrote about being stopped and harassed by the police. In another article, a university student from New Brunswick identified herself as "a nonviolent pacifist" and wrote about her anxiety at getting swept up with Black Bloc protesters—only to realize that the police were the real source of violence that day. "Because of [the Black Bloc's] presence at the protests, I felt protected," she wrote, "I felt safe." In another article, a member of a "bikeshevik" caravan that rode from Montreal to Quebec described his encounters with the police—and opined about the civic infrastructure the Quebec government could build with the $100 million it spent on security for the summit.

In the days following the Quebec City mobilizations, Maude Barlow, who had been at the protests ("hit time and again with tear gas"), reflected on the "tough questions" that journalists had asked her in the aftermath of the mobilization. In an article written for *The Nation* that was republished on rabble, Barlow wrote:

> Where is the real violence? Let's talk about that. Well, I say the real violence lies behind that wall, with the thirty-four political leaders and their spin-doctors and their corporate friends who bought their way in, sleeping in five-star hotels and eating in five-star restaurants and thinking they can run the world by themselves. Well, I have news for them – there are more of us than there are of them, and we say, "No!"
>
> The question isn't what I am going to do with angry young people. The question should be put to Prime Minister Jean Chrétien and President George Bush and all the other leaders here to promote the extension of this toxic economy: What are you going to do with them? It is your market economy, with its emphasis on ruthless competition and the wanton destruction of the natural world, that has created such deep wellsprings of anger in such large sections of today's youth, and it is you, the political leaders, so beholden to the private interests who put you in power, who must be held accountable.

That anger would go unresolved, and it remains unresolved. A similar rage has millions of people pouring into the streets today to demand an end to the state-sanctioned murder of Black and Indigenous people and people of colour, and an end to an economy that prioritizes police gear over personal protective equipment. Mainstream news media has seldom reported in any real way on the roots of this anger. Then, as now, news cameras zero in on looting, rioting, and burning. Where is the platform for Barlow's "angry young people" in Quebec? Where is the platform for today's activists in the streets?

The answer has always been: independent media.

It was from this hope and anger that rabble was born. And stories of hope and anger also lie at the heart of this book: a collection of articles pulled from rabble's archive over the past twenty years and published on the occasion of the website's twentieth anniversary. *Everything on (the) Line* features one story from rabble's archives for every year since 2001, divided into four sections (2001–5, 2006–10, 2011–14, and 2015–20), with each section introduced by an original essay reflecting from our present moment.

One of the first issues that the two of us bonded over in our work as part-time editors at rabble was the site's sprawling archive. Work published on the site has been anthologized before, in occasional "Best of rabble" books that compiled highlights from specific years in the site's history. But after nearly twenty years, several website redesigns, and much staffing changeover, the site's archive was nearly impossible to access online. Half of the material, from the site's early years, was stored on a password-protected old website. Even on the current site, a reader looking to find stories from the Occupy movement, for example, could hardly use the search function to find a set of relevant stories. Knowledge of what had been published in years past was stored in many different people's memories; to know where to look and what to look for, you needed a guide. At first, we tried to remedy the problem in the present by streamlining the keywords we used to tag new stories and content on the site. But as rabble's twentieth anniversary approached, we began to feel that a new approach was necessary.

An anniversary is always an occasion for reflection, but it was the world around us that served as the real prompt for this book. The racialized impact of corporate power, climate breakdown, and a rotten neoliberal consensus was breaking down. We also saw a glimmer of hope: in a resurging political left, in young people organizing in their schools and communities, in the movement for Black lives. How could we build on this hope? How could we turn it into power—the power to chart a different course and build a just world? Where had past movements, like the antiglobalization movement, failed, and what could be done differently? We were both children when rabble was founded at the tail end of the antiglobalization movement. It is one thing to seek an intellectual understanding of past political and social movements and quite another to read dispatches from the very people organizing those movements. To grapple with our present moment, we wanted to hear from activists themselves.

Rabble's archive is massive, with hundreds of thousands of stories, and there was no way to tell every story or catalogue every voice ever published. This book does not purport to engage with every story in the rabble archive, nor is it an organizational history of rabble—though the final chapter, written by the site's longtime publisher, Kim Elliott, and current board president, Matthew Adams, offers their perspective on the site's development. Our aim, instead, was to select articles from rabble's archive and put them into conversation with contemporary essays to help readers reflect on the social movements that challenged capitalism, racism, settler colonialism, and patriarchy over the past two decades.

This book represents our collaborative effort to revisit some of the ideas and stories in rabble's archive and to offer snapshots of the grassroots struggles that precipitated our current moment—a moment where, to quote Leah Gazan in the conversation found in this book's last section, "we have everything on the line."

A New Kind of Space

In 2001, it became immediately clear to rabble's founders that an appetite for stories of social movement struggle existed in Canada: rabble went from zero to forty thousand hits per day just days after launching. As rabble co-founder Mark Surman noted on the site's tenth anniversary in 2011, this was a pivotal period in the history of the web. "We were actually at a point where 98 percent of the internet was all viewed through Microsoft," Surman said. "We were at the end of the dot com bubble crash." The internet had yet to become the mainstream for news publishing. At the same time, there were many social movements in Canada looking for new ways to share and broadcast their aims, and rabble seized on this potential; as Surman said, it took the internet from being a "thing" and sought to transform it into a new kind of "space."

As with the independent mediamakers that predated rabble, contributors to the project understood that independent media offered more than a journalistic alternative to mainstream news coverage of protests and movements. Its founders and supporters hoped rabble, as a space, would serve as critical movement infrastructure in the fight against corporate globalization. As April Glaser explained on the twentieth anniversary of the Indymedia Network in *Logic Magazine*, the independent media movement understood that "a movement to oppose globalized, networked capital needed to be globalized and networked too. And that meant getting online."

What did it mean, then, to be a "space" on the internet? For one, it meant that from the get-go, rabble's journalism was participatory and unfiltered—without compromising on journalistic rigour. "I was reporting from the [Quebec] streets calling my reports into our editor [and rabble co-founder] Jude MacDonald who wrote them up," Rebick recalled about the Summit of the Americas. It was a news site that not only reported on, but was also embedded in, activist movements. Because of that, rabble also blurred the lines between contributors and readers: the site's discussion board (later named babble) was one of its most lively features early on, commanding up to 60 percent of the site's traffic.

In its early days, rabble shuttled between being a space for sharing activist news and one where debates between social movements played out. In one article about street theatre at the Quebec City protests, Rebick wrote about the "medieval bloc," a protest group formed by the Deconstructionist Institute for Surreal Topology (DIST) that had built a six-metre long catapult (with funding from Rebick herself) and hauled it to the barricade, hurling stuffed toys across the police lines. Police arrested activist Jaggi Singh and charged him with possession of a weapon. In an irreverent press release published on rabble several days later, DIST insisted that Singh was not involved with their street theatre because "his sense of humour does not meet the rigorous standards required by DIST." Still, police refused to release Singh, and a petition on rabble that demanded his release garnered over six thousand signatures. In addition to being a gathering place for activists to discuss tactics and strategies, rabble was a vehicle for self-expression and community-building, an activist space in its own right.

As an online space, rabble was also unencumbered by the infrastructure and costs of print media—and thus able, and willing, to evolve. One of the site's earliest pivots came just five months after its founding, when on September 11, 2001, the attacks on the World Trade Center in New York City changed global politics forever. A surge in online traffic driven by people looking for news about the attacks caused the websites of several mainstream media outlets to crash, which drove readers to rabble. Jude MacDonald recalled in 2011 that the site's editors put a babble thread up on the front page to which people could post verified news about the attacks.

The 9/11 attacks became a hinge event that the US and its allies, Canada included, used to justify the implementation of authoritarian security measures at home and military intervention and human rights violations overseas. The aftermath of 9/11 made reluctant activists of many caught up in these "security" measures. Monia Mazigh was one. In 2002, Mazigh was visiting her native Tunisia with her two young children when her husband, Maher Arar, was arrested in New York. Arar spent over a year in American and then Syrian custody. Mazigh's essay in this book, co-written with her daughter Barâa Arar, details Mazigh's efforts to secure her husband's release and the long-term effects of his rendition on their family.

Arar and Mazigh's essay opens this book's first section, which covers work published on rabble between 2001 and 2005 and focuses on the security measures implemented after 9/11 and their effects on Muslims and other people detained under suspicion of terrorism. The mental and emotional costs of such detention reverberate beyond the individual, as emphasized in Mazigh and Arar's essay and Maha Zimmo's article on Sophie Harkat. Zimmo's article, written in 2005, describes the arrest of Harkat's husband, Mohamed, on suspicion of ties to Al-Qaeda. For nearly two decades, the federal government has sought to deport Mohamed Harkat—who for years has been living under draconian house arrest—to Algeria.

As the arrests of Harkat and others illustrate, the Canadian government frequently fell in line with US security demands. The mainstream media often fell in line, too. In 2001, mainstream pundits lambasted sociologist Sunera Thobani for questioning the US response to 9/11. As Lynn Coady's article on Thobani illustrates, several prominent media outlets, including the *Globe and Mail,* ran editorials suggesting it was inappropriate to question the spirit of retribution that marked government responses to the attacks.

It's easy to see 9/11 as a turning point in contemporary global history, but of course, the seeds of much of what happened afterward were planted long before. The other articles found in the book's first section situate the events of this period in a much longer history of Western imperialism. Carlos A. Torres's 2003 article is an important reminder about the "other" September 11: the 1973 US-supported military coup that marked the beginning of Augusto Pinochet's seventeen-year dictatorship. Duncan Cameron's 2004 article on Canada's response to US plans for missile defence criticizes our government's reluctance to stand up to our militaristic southern neighbour. And Erin George's 2002 series of profiles of protesters at the demonstration against the G8 Summit in Calgary features an eclectic array of voices—a sixty-one-year-old nun from Rimouski, a high school student, a member of the Canadian Auto Workers' local 199, a disability rights activist, a labour leader, a street nurse, an activist from Soweto, and others—united around resistance to corporate globalization and capitalism. George's series represents the best of rabble's archives and demonstrates the power of an activist-oriented platform.

While a policy of US appeasement has long marked Canadian governments of all political stripes, the year 2006 marked a major shift in domestic politics. That year, the minority government of Canadian Prime Minister Stephen Harper ended the Liberal Party's thirteen-year reign. While Harper wouldn't achieve a majority government until 2011, his election nonetheless signalled a shift towards neoliberal economic policy in Canada.

This shift is the focus of the book's second section, which covers the years 2006–10. A key plank of Harper's economic policy involved ramping up resource extraction across the country, which required access to

Indigenous lands. As Russell Diabo details in his introductory essay to this section, the Harper government's policies boiled down to turning sovereign Indigenous nations into what Diabo calls "ethnic municipalities": political units fully incorporated into the Canadian nation-state yet subordinate to provincial and federal levels of government. This, as Diabo points out, runs counter to both the spirit of treaties between Canada and First Nations and the recognition of Indigenous rights in the Canadian constitution. What if Indigenous communities don't consent to resource extraction on their lands? What if First Nations want to be seen as political communities in their own right rather than defined by their relationship with the Canadian state? Diabo, a longtime activist and First Nations policy analyst and a member of the Mohawk Nation at Kahnawake, has been grappling with these questions for decades.

The articles in this section of the book speak to the social movements that arose and grew in response to Harper's "Indian" policy during this period. Between 1962 and 1970, Dryden Chemicals dumped mercury into the English-Wabigoon river system, on which multiple Ojibwe communities rely for their water supply. Dryden's dumping led to catastrophic levels of mercury poisoning in these communities, which in turn began to organize (with the support of Indigenous and non-Indigenous allies) to hold the company and provincial and federal governments to account. As Carmelle Wolfson discusses in her 2008 article, activism around Grassy Narrows led to a widespread Indigenous solidarity movement that featured a three-day gathering and camp-out at Queen's Park. Relatedly, Corvin Russell's 2010 article examines how the federal and Quebec governments sought to dismantle independent forms of Indigenous governance in the Algonquin community of Barriere Lake. During this period, rabble covered activist groups like Barriere Lake Solidarity, of which Russell was a member, which sought to hold governments to account and stop the attempted assimilation of Indigenous communities.

Rabble's coverage in this period wasn't restricted to Indigenous rights movements unfolding within Canada's borders; in 2006, the site published a dispatch by Emilie Teresa Smith, who had rushed to Oaxaca, Mexico as the police began cracking down on protestors there. A teacher's strike, which had begun months earlier over school funding in rural Indigenous communities, provoked increasingly violent government responses. Her article is a reminder that state violence against Indigenous-led social movements stretches across North America and of the important solidarity networks that have developed between activists in Canada and those abroad.

Beyond issues of land, Indigenous activists in this period also drew attention to the underreported and underinvestigated disappearance of Indigenous women and girls across the country. This issue came to a head during the trial of Robert Pickton, the serial murderer who is thought to have killed at least twenty-seven women, many of them Indigenous. As Amber Dean writes in her 2007 piece on Pickton's trial, the families of these disappeared women sought to correct the mainstream media's mischaracterization of the women, who were often described as "prostitutes" and "drug addicts." Dean's article is another example of how rabble continued to hold mainstream media to account in the mid-aughts.

Alongside the Indigenous activist movements that grew between 2006 and 2010 occurred broader shifts in the global economy. The 2008 recession, triggered by the bursting of the US housing bubble, led to years of austerity measures in Canada and around the world. The 2008 recession magnified existing inequalities and highlighted systemic issues with global capitalism. During this period, writers on the left asked us to imagine a more just, egalitarian world, which is the subject of Murray Dobbin's 2009 piece on prosperity without growth. "We need, on the Left, to once again become the source of Big Ideas," Dobbin writes: for a wealth tax, a comprehensive climate policy, and a social world built around conviviality and collective health rather than work and consumption.

Several of these "Big Ideas" fuelled movements that arose after 2008, drawing attention to the yawning inequalities revealed and created by the recession and ensuing austerity. The 2010 Vancouver Olympics, promoted as a nationalist celebration and an economic opportunity for Canada's Western metropolis, led to evictions and rent hikes in the city's poorest neighbourhoods. In response, a group of activists set up the Olympic Tent Village in the city's Downtown Eastside to draw attention to the housing precarity that had been worsened by the Games. Four months later, thousands of protestors filled the streets of Toronto during the G20 summit, and an overzealous police response led to the largest mass arrest in Canadian history. Writers from rabble were there, too, reporting on the protests from the streets and the designated press area.

For Harper's Conservative government, the years following the 2008 financial crisis provided an opportunity to usher in a new wave of privatization, deregulation, and austerity. While Canadian banks had enjoyed a secret bailout to the tune of $114 billion, people in Canada saw their wages continue to decline—as they had for thirty years—and the quality of their public services, from health care to public transit, eroded. Ten years after rabble's launch at the last major antiglobalization protest, the world economy was in freefall. A new word emerged to characterize the anxiousness that had pervaded near every aspect of society: precarity. In his introductory essay to the third section of this book, former rabble opinions editor Michael Stewart describes how Harper's precarity program—waged on political and rhetorical planes—nearly tore apart Canada's already threadbare social fabric.

The stories from rabble's archives featured in the third section of this book cover the social movements—led by migrant workers, organized labour, young people of colour, students and Indigenous women—that rose up to challenge Harper, precarity, and Canada's unacceptable status quo. In 2011, Jesse McLaren covered NDP leader Jack Layton's propulsion on the Orange Wave into the official opposition, which represented, for many rabble readers, a sense that the political needle was shifting. But the NDP's newfound political power would not change Canada's economic reality overnight, nor would the party prevent the devastating wave of austerity that Harper and the provinces would unleash in the years to come. In 2012, Christopher Majka analyzed the political and economic context of the tuition hikes that had hundreds of thousands of young students and workers pour into the streets and organize a province-wide strike against provincial austerity measures in Quebec. The Idle No More movement followed quickly on the heels of the Quebec student strikes. Beginning in November of 2012 in response to an omnibus bill that would dismantle protections for Canada's waterways, Idle No More quickly grew into a broadly coalitional Indigenous sovereignty movement. As longtime rabble contributor Pamela Palmater writes in her 2013 article on Idle No

More, the movement "inspired the most oppressed peoples to stand up and exercise their voices."

Beyond their attempted erosion of Indigenous rights, Harper's government created massive upheavals for workers and organized labour. As unions went on the defensive, fighting the tide of layoffs, privatization, and private capital, corporations, emboldened by Harper's corporate tax cuts, grew the "gig" economy. All the while, Harper and the Conservatives deftly reapportioned blame onto migrant workers, writes Stewart. Then-Minister for Employment Jason Kenney turned the Temporary Foreign Workers Program (TFWP) into the target of xenophobic, antimigrant ire. In 2014, Syed Hussan of the Migrant Workers Alliance for Change, a group that would later be on the frontlines of migrant justice organizing during the coronavirus pandemic, wrote about Canada's "corporate-driven" immigration system. The social movements of these years built the foundation of a sometimes undetectable, but seismic shift: the widespread sense that another world is not just possible but, as Stewart writes, "within our grasp."

Electoral politics may seem like the clearest benchmark by which to measure such political changes. But Canada's broken first-past-the-post electoral system can hardly be said to represent voters' political sensibilities accurately. Nevertheless, after a decade of anti-Harper organizing, voters in Canada—many casting so-called "strategic" ballots—propelled Justin Trudeau's Liberal Party to victory in the 2015 federal election. Karl Nerenberg, rabble's parliamentary reporter, reported on how Liberals, campaigning even to the left of the NDP, which had tacked to the centre under then-leader Tom Mulcair, made promises of "real change" and "sunny ways." The party would ultimately fail to keep those promises, as Nora Loreto writes in her introduction to the final section of this book, which features stories originally published on rabble from 2015 through 2020.

In her chapter, Loreto, an author, activist, and longtime rabble contributor, details how activists redeployed radical tactics to organize against anti-Black racism, late-stage capitalism, and resource extraction. The Black Lives Matter movement was one of the most powerful movements to come of age during these years. It took on the pernicious, systemic anti-Black racism woven into every aspect of Canadian society. As Mark Brown writes in his 2016 article on the movement,

> Whether they are blocking Toronto's Allen Expressway, camping out at the Toronto Police Headquarters or engaging in some other creative form of protest in order to get the message heard, history will not soon forget the sisters and brothers of BLM-TO who compelled a society to look at its own privilege.

History did not forget. Trudeau tried to paint himself as an ally to this movement, marching in the 2016 Pride parade where BLM-TO was featured as the honoured group, and taking the knee during a June 2020 antiracism protest in Ottawa. But Black Lives Matter activists would have none of it; during an anti-Islamophobia rally in 2017, a founder of Black Lives Matter Toronto condemned Trudeau's hypocritical stance on immigration, labelling him a "white supremacist terrorist." Two years later, when multiple photos of Trudeau in Blackface emerged during the 2019 federal election campaign, Trudeau's progressive veneer crumbled for good.

Indigenous land defenders also ramped up organizing in opposition to the Trudeau government's unyielding support for the fossil fuel industry. In 2017, Erin Despard wrote about the Tiny House Warriors, antipipeline activists from the Secwepemc Nation who were building small wooden-frame houses along the planned path for the Trans Mountain Pipeline expansion project. Climate activists—the "valve turners" Brent Patterson wrote about on rabble in 2018—literally shut off pipelines across Turtle Island to call attention to Canada's failure to act on climate breakdown.

At the same time, young people have reinvigorated the climate justice movement and have begun to drum up popular support for climate solutions like a radical Green New Deal. For climate strikers, who have watched as Jeff Bezos was projected to become the world's first trillionaire by 2026, the neoliberal refrain of "how will you pay for it?" has become a laughable relic of an earlier era. The Green New Deal framework draws an explicit link between climate breakdown and capitalism to assert that the only real solutions to the climate crisis are ones that simultaneously undo systems of patriarchy, racism, and settler colonialism. It may turn out to be one of the most potent climate concepts of the decade.

In this period, feminists made widespread use of hashtag activism. But so long as whiteness, heterosexuality, and cisness remain the mainstream feminist frame, the movement will remain "slippery and toothless," as Loreto writes—even as a stealthy war on women is waged in Canada in the form of cuts to reproductive health care, conservative encroachment on the right and access to abortion, and rising child-care costs, all of which Antonia Zerbisias detailed for rabble in 2019. The feminism of the future, on which we stake our politics *and* this book, has no room for trans-exclusionary radical feminists, white supremacy, dog-whistle politics, or hatred. Essential to radical feminism is the vision of transformative justice that Reakash Walters and Rachel Zellars outlined on rabble in their 2020 essay about police abolition. Building effective feminist movements will be a matter of linking feminist action with the fight against anti-Black racism, transphobia and transmisogyny, and capitalism. It will certainly require a lot more than hashtags.

As Loreto puts it, the story of the years 2015 to 2020 was of "real change" meeting "radical tactics." Today, as we collectively stare down a pandemic, it remains unclear how that meeting will play out. The critiques of corporate globalization and capitalism levied by the antiglobalization movement that birthed rabble in 2001 are as prescient as ever in our current moment. Will disaster capitalists exploit the economic crisis induced by the pandemic to consolidate power? Will protesters taking to the streets to demand police and prison abolition finally triumph over PR-savvy politicians perverting their message? Will militant social movements harness this moment of opportunity to build a better, more just world? Will we see liberation in our lifetime?

This book is not a comprehensive history of the past twenty years of Canadian politics or social movement history. There are many stories we don't tell in these pages: the housing activists whose efforts have exposed, again and again, the need for a national housing policy; countless struggles led by the labour movement; the community workers who set up safe injection sites in the face of government foot-dragging on this country's opioid crisis; the victories won by LGBTQ2S+ movements (including the

2005 legalization of same-sex marriage) and the dangers still faced by members of these communities, especially by queer people of colour; the Free Palestine and Boycott, Divestment, and Sanctions (BDS) movements against Israeli apartheid; the net neutrality fight and movements against the corporate capture of the internet; and many, many more. Looking back at rabble's archive, we observed how certain ideas and modes of discourse seem antiquated just years after publishing. As with all journalistic writing, the stories republished in this collection are each rooted in a particular moment and tied to the contours of a particular public conversation. In these stories, a reader will come across predictions that did not turn out to be true, perspectives and words presented as widely accepted that no longer are, and certainties about the way the world works that recent history has undermined. In all of this, there are lessons: about how we make sense of the world around us, about how processes of sense-making change over time, and about the limitations of journalistic analysis itself.

The last section of this book is dedicated to thinking about the past and future of independent media. Readers will find a brief snapshot of rabble as an organization written by board president Matthew Adams and publisher Kim Elliott. This is followed by a panel conversation we held in April 2020 with Judy Rebick and two Indigenous activists, Eriel Tchekwie Deranger, a leader in the climate justice space, and NDP Member of Parliament Leah Gazan that touches on their personal stories of struggle and hope and the role of independent media in social movements.

The conclusion of *Everything on (the) Line*, written by Phillip Dwight Morgan, offers the writer's reflections on the coronavirus pandemic and racial justice and outlines a framework for the future of independent media. Whatever happens, we will need hope, and we see alternative media as a space for hope to take root and grow. We will need spaces—online and offline—to debate and communicate, to chart new ideas, tactics, and strategies that build on that hope and transform the world as we know it. Over the past two decades, the liberatory possibilities of the internet that activists seized upon when rabble was founded have faded, as corporate behemoths and social media platforms came to capture cyberspace. But the task of building alternative, independent, and activist-run digital spaces has only become more urgent. As people organize to take on racial capitalism and ecofascism, alternative mediamakers might do well to recall the task as our predecessors once saw it: to sustain critical movement infrastructure. And infrastructure, like any tool, needs continual maintenance, remodelling, and reimagining. It is our wish that the new generation of activists challenging disaster capitalism in a post-pandemic era will harness this infrastructure, correct past mistakes, and sharpen new forms of independent media into tools capable of piercing systems of power and creating new worlds. We hope that the next generation of activists will make rabble their own.

2001–
2005

Section 1: From Antiglobalization to National Security

Collateral

Monia Mazigh and Barâa Arar

My mother often tells the story I repeated as a child of my father's rescue plan. I thought we should find a helicopter, fly to Syria, and bring my dad home to Ottawa. Clearly, as a kid, I did not understand artificial borders, helicopter piloting, or geographic distance. But children are not supposed to know what any of that means.

"What were you doing that day?" journalists kept asking me. They wanted my words for the story they were writing. As if a young mother with an eight-month-old infant and a four-year-old preschooler can remember what she has done or eaten the previous day. It wasn't even a question asked by other parents at playgroup or by a nosy neighbour. It was asked over and over by journalists, a new class of total strangers, after my husband was arrested by the American authorities in New York. And the day they were asking about was not any day in the year. It was September 11, 2001. The day that the twin towers of the World Trade Center were attacked and collapsed, and the day the world swirled into the War on Terror declared a few weeks later by US president George W. Bush.

But I didn't have the privilege to reply, "I can't remember." As a Muslim woman with a husband arrested by the American authorities under suspicion of terrorist activities in the wake of 9/11, I didn't have the audacity to tell them to get lost. I didn't have the luxury of looking them in the eyes and asking them: "Do you remember what you were doing that day?" I had to dig into my memory and keep turning that painful screw in my brain and revisiting the past twelve months, day after day, week after week, month after month. Trying to remember, trying to put together the pieces of the puzzle, trying to make sense of the Kafkaesque journey into which I had been catapulted.

That became my life after my husband, Maher Arar, a Canadian citizen of Syrian descent, was arrested on September 26, 2002.

This was the life of a wife looking for impossible answers. It was the life of a mother who tried to give her two young children an impression of normalcy and preserve what was left of their innocent lives while thinking about how to make ends meet and, above all, find justice for my husband, arrested by the American authorities, abandoned by the Canadian government, imprisoned and tortured by the Syrian regime.

But even answering the journalists' questions didn't make my husband spontaneously reappear.

Allowing those hungry eyes to feast on my private life didn't bring me any closer to freeing my husband from the dungeon he found himself in. Even after telling them that that morning, I was four months pregnant, in the kitchen of my suburban Ottawa home, with Radio-Canada on as usual, preparing breakfast for my daughter and most likely thinking about a deadline for my research work at the University of Ottawa, my words weren't enough for the insistent journalists or the apathetic politicians involved in my husband's case.

Perhaps they were expecting me to tell them that I was in my basement, concocting some dangerous recipe to terrorize people, or reassure them I was waiting for instructions from my husband to tell me what to do with my day.

I have a hard time remembering moments from my childhood. I don't remember 9/11 like other people my age. I was five. Not young enough to justify misremembering but not old enough to understand the implications of that date, both politically and for my personal life.

What I vividly remember is the footage of the planes crashing into the twin towers, the one that aired on CNN and every other major network, for what seemed to be eternity. If you close your eyes and picture 9/11, this is probably what you remember. It's a wide shot, taken from afar, as the towers burn and eventually implode. When I think of 9/11, that is what I first think of.

But that is a sanitized memory. It is an attempt to objectify the event, distancing myself from it, pushing away what it meant for my life. The American news media successfully mythologized the event so that all of us have the same image of that day.

Ironically, that day, on 9/11, my husband was in the US, in Silicon Valley, with his American colleague selling MATLAB, a software created by an American company named MathWorks. He worked for MathWorks, and his job as a telecommunication engineer took him and his colleagues across the US and around the world to convince tech and engineering companies to buy their products.

But on September 26, 2002, all his trips came abruptly to a halt.

The Americans arrested him in New York at JFK Airport, interrogated him, strip-searched him, blindfolded him, shackled him, and sent him to the Metropolitan Detention Center, where the lights were kept on for twenty-three hours a day. Then, two weeks later, they drove him in the middle of the night to an airport in New Jersey, where a ghost plane was waiting for him.

Ghost planes belong to private corporations subcontracted by the US government to render "suspected terrorists" to other countries where they can make them disappear, torture them, or indefinitely detain them. So, even if these planes physically exist, they are "off the radar" of institutions like the International Air Transport Association. In a nutshell, they cannot be held responsible for breaking international law. They fly in the sky unbothered by any extra scrutiny; they do the "dirty job" of governments.

Very few people have heard about these planes. In Hollywood movies, the war on terror is usually described as a story of heroes. Brave and handsome American men loaded with machine guns and helped by drones and sexy blonde women in their mission to kill as many terrorist brown men as possible and save as many oppressed Muslim women as possible. Like the oppression of those who were impacted by these post-9/11 "national security measures," the men who were sent to prison for crimes they didn't commit, the women who lost their male relatives to torture, waterboarding, killing, the children who missed their fathers and suffered in silence at the sight of their overwhelmed mothers, my husband, my kids and I were part of one of these untold dark stories.

I rarely talk about my father's case. Not because I am ashamed, but because telling the story is exhausting. Whenever I know I am going to meet new people, especially mutual friends, I ask someone to fill them in beforehand. Casually mentioning your father was falsely accused and incarcerated is not a fun party trick.

I wrack my brain for memories from my father's absence. I remember living in a small two-bedroom apartment on the first floor of a rental community in Ottawa. I remember my maternal grandmother, always around, almost omnipresent, ready to give me an afternoon snack. I remember my brother in his highchair, crying until he fell asleep. I remember my father was absent, but it was a passive absence—a void. I felt my mother's absence more definitively. Whereas I did not see my father consecutively, my mother came to me in pieces during the time she was fighting for his release. My mom became a single mother abruptly and unwillingly. I now know that it is her education, her perseverance, and her sharpness that helped soften the blow. My mom's steadfastness and resistance to the system is exactly why we did not become absolute victims of it.

I went to school like everyone else, had birthday parties, and cake, and presents like everyone else. At the time, I don't think I registered that I was different. As an adult, I know that forces far more powerful than a five-year-old girl can understand were shaping a big part of my and my family's story.

I did not yet know we were becoming collateral damage.

Neoliberalism isn't only about markets and corporations. It isn't only about goods and commodities. In a sense, neoliberalism commodifies people. It treats them like merchandise. Especially if these people are the "others," those who were declared "enemy combatants," those who happen to be caught in the cracks of this war on terror, those who, if one day found innocent, will still be called collateral damage. Neoliberalism's ultimate goal is the erasure of our humanity. With noble targets like efficiency and profits, it creeps under our layers of democratic institutions to erase the tracks of the abuse conducted by governments.

So, what happens to you and your family when you become collateral damage in the war on terror?

You disappear. First, physically and later, morally. My husband disappeared. For weeks I didn't know his whereabouts. No one from the Canadian government could answer my question: where is my husband? Then, when he reappeared, he was in prison in Syria. However, I was never told where exactly in Syria, the name of the prison, the precise location. Those details may seem unimportant, but for a family in darkness, they can be a vital source of light. When the "system" eliminates these details and prevents you from even knowing the name of the prison where your husband is and its location, in reality, it is sending you an encrypted message. Your husband, or your father or your son, doesn't matter in this world. He is worthless. And by extension, you are worthless too. You don't deserve any answers, even the most basic ones.

I have moments of lucidity, but what I remember is not ideal. In the days following my father's arrest, we—my mom, brother, and I—were stranded in Tunisia, waiting for paperwork so my newborn baby brother could come back to Canada with us. My father's whereabouts were yet unclear. This was before Twitter and text messaging, and everything moved slowly. You could go hours without hearing from a loved one, days even.

My mom was busy at the Ministry of the Interior in Tunisia trying to get an authorization to leave needed for my brother's temporary passport. How do you explain that the father of your child cannot be present to sign because you don't know where he is? My mother was late picking me up from the neighbour's house, where I was staying. They told me to eat spicy couscous they prepared, and I was upset because I don't like spicy food. I remember the moment I saw my mom and ran into her safe arms. I am not the only one with these stories. All children experience abandonment, but not for the same reasons.

My sixth birthday was the one I spent without my father. It was a bone-chilling night in February. My homemade birthday cake, strawberry shortcake with chocolate on top, was on top of our fridge. Someone tried to open the freezer, and the cake collapsed onto the floor. I remember everyone scrambling to fix it, tears welling up in my eyes. My paternal uncle, who resembled my father in face and figure, was with us that night. Maybe he thought he would be a stand-in. Maybe he was just being an uncle.

Just like with my birthday cake, the people closest to my family scrambled to make everything okay. My mother tried to maintain a sense of normalcy. Parents around the world hope to do that for their children in times of uncertainty. Sometimes I wonder if that is helpful or destructive. Because what we lived through was most definitely not normal.

The war on terror and the national security agenda that accompanied it in the US and Canada had two sides, both ugly. The obvious side: brutal and visible, where governments would go fight the "terrorists" on the ground, torture them, and kill them. Even if Canada didn't send troops into the Iraq War launched by the US after 9/11, the federal government still sought to appease the belligerent US on other matters like missile defence.

But there is another insidious side to this, equally brutal but not visible to the public eye. One that many governments conducted against their own citizens (or sometimes refugees or permanent residents) of Muslim faith with apparently legal tools: antiterrorism legislation. Many of these citizens were stripped of their constitutional rights, so even if they still physically exist, they don't enjoy their rights anymore, they become second-class citizens.

They become subhuman.

In order to prove that you exist, that your humanity does matter, and that you deserve to be noticed, you have to make noise. A lot of noise.

I came to that conclusion by trial and error. I started to speak out. It was my turn to ask them, too: "Where is my husband?" "Is he alive?" "When will you bring him back home?" I asked those questions at vigils, in letters to my Member of Parliament, at meetings with politicians, in protests in front of the US Embassy in Ottawa, and in front of the Prime Minister's office on Elgin Street, in phone calls to some journalists, who by then became familiar faces.

In return, I didn't get straight answers. I heard, "keep a low profile, as your activism might hurt your husband's case." I heard, "he is Syrian and is now in Syria so there is nothing we can do about it." I heard, "get a life." I became someone who disturbs the government's official position. Someone whose presence is unwelcomed.

Wearing a headscarf had made me unwelcome in Tunis, my hometown. It was the 1990s, and the police regime of that time launched a witch-hunt against all signs of religiosity. Though long considered part of Tunisia's religious and cultural identity, the headscarf came to be seen as a sign of backwardness, religious extremism, and violence. My decision to immigrate to Canada was motivated by this persecution that made policemen arrest women wearing headscarves in public spaces, snatching their scarves from their heads, humiliating them, and sending them to a police station to sign a formal commitment not to wear one anymore.

A few months before I graduated and moved to Canada, the director of my university called and informed me that wearing a headscarf was no longer allowed and that I would be prevented from entering campus.

In Canada, I thought that I would be accepted. Rather, I was simply tolerated. My visibility bothered some people who perceived my hijab as a sign of women's oppression. That was until my husband was arrested, and then my hijab became a sign of double oppression: male oppression and Islamist affiliation.

I am not saying that Islamophobia didn't exist before 9/11. But when Muslim issues become more and more visible, first through the 1991 Gulf War and later post-9/11, the general population in the US and Canada, helped by the media, discovered the "Muslim threat" and started reacting to it. They reacted first with fear and later with hate.

The national security measures enacted after 9/11 erased your individuality. If you fulfil a number of criteria, you become awfully close to being a terrorist. To my brother and me, he was the father who gave us piggyback rides. But to the state, to the narrow-minded agenda of the war on terror, he is a bearded, Middle Eastern engineer. That immediately made him suspicious. He starts to look awfully like all the men screaming "Allahu Akbar" on American television. Superficial elements of your identity supplement your rights and any commitment to due process.

The national security agenda that unfolded immediately after 9/11 in the US was copied by Canada with Bill C-36, which became the

Anti-terrorism Act. This gave the population a false sense of security. Because security comes with a price. Not only the price of tanks, guns, and military equipment. Usually, the most vulnerable in a society pay that price with their lives and their own security. The whole idea of "us versus them" intensified. That led to the creation of special laws: antiterrorism legislation. The argument goes as follows: for special people, we create special laws. The whole agenda of national security is built on racist and Islamophobic ideas about Muslims. Because Muslims are described as exceptionally violent and barbaric, it would be implicitly accepted by the legislator and later by the population that the government brings exceptionally harsh laws to spy on them, preemptively arrest them, and ultimately punish them.

The creation of these laws perpetuated many myths around Islam and Muslims. Worse, Islamophobia got normalized.

In November 2002, Diane Ablonczy, an MP from the Canadian Alliance, stood up in the House of Commons falsely describing my husband as a businessman (he was an engineer) of forty years of age (he was thirty-two) with an "Al-Qaeda link" (he was never accused by any government of terrorist activities), praising the US for arresting him, and blaming Canada for not "uncovering" him first. What explanation can be given for that "fake news"? In 2015, Ablonczy was promoted to Minister of State for Foreign Affairs in the Harper government.

Even when my husband was freed after a long year of unjust imprisonment without trial or charge, my battle wasn't over. After his return to Canada, some journalists, using anonymous sources, wrote about my husband's case, doubting he was a victim of torture and insinuating he was not innocent. While these journalists were interested in boosting their careers, their false claims were destroying what was left of my husband's reputation and our life as a family. Once again, we had to prove our humanity to the general public. We had to stay calm and nice. We had to prove our allegiance to Canada.

It didn't matter that we came willingly to Canada. It didn't matter that we studied hard, got degrees from the best Canadian universities, worked hard and paid our taxes, and raised our family in Canada. None of this mattered when we were called terrorists. We were examined through the lens of our Islamness, and the result was that we always had to prove we belonged.

But there was worse. After 9/11, the Canadian government intensified its use of an already existing procedure called security certificates. The government targeted permanent residents and refugees deemed by secret intelligence agencies to represent a national security threat. Once a "suspect" is served with a security certificate, he will be imminently deported to his homeland. This is how five Muslim Arab men came to be indefinitely detained for years in what came to be known as Guantanamo North.

Recently, a psychiatrist asked me if most of the memories from my childhood are happy. I couldn't answer him. On the one hand, I remember learning to ride a bike when we lived in a townhouse in Ottawa's west end. In every flashback, I imagine it was sunny, and my mom was waving to me from our front porch. In the days after my father's arrest, I remember biking around in the lot in front of my grandfather's house in Tunisia. Was I aware of what was going on? Or did I peddle ferociously like every other five-year-old hoping to do tricks or maybe even fly?

The day we saw my father again is imprinted in my mind in fragments. I do not trust my own recollection of it. I think the phone rang early in the morning, my mother picked up, and her reaction to the voice on the other side was confirmation of his release. I don't remember joy, but I remember relief. As if everyone in our two-bedroom apartment finally sighed.

We went to Montreal as a family, accompanied by some activists who had been volunteering to free my father. At the Montreal airport, we were given a room to wait in until the plane landed. I have a vague image of my father coming down a long hallway, his figure much thinner than when he left, his clothes tattered, a vision of vulnerability. I don't know if I qualify that as a happy memory, but it was a chance to rebuild a life that was stolen from us.

I joined the fight for justice for these men detained under security certificates. I came to know most of the families, their supporters, and their friends. My suffering that started with the disappearance of my husband was supposed to end when he came back home, but it didn't.

It metamorphosed and embraced the continuum traced by successive Canadian governments in perpetuating the injustice and the scrutiny that enveloped the lives of Muslims in this land.

Mohamed Harkat, Adil Charkaoui, Mohamed Mahjoub, Mahmoud Jaballah, Hassan Almrei. All of them were served with security certificates.

The list became longer with other names affected by other discriminating measures: Abdullah Al Malki, Ahmed Al Maati, Muayed Nurredine, Abu Soufiane Abdelrazik, and many other Canadians detained and tortured abroad. The fight took the form of protest, advocacy, and writing. It became part of the new "me." The one that awoke when they imprisoned my husband then grew up through a decade of systemic Islamophobia.

For years growing up, strangers would approach me and say, "You're Maher's daughter? Right?" I would nod, upset that the public adopted this as my identifier but passively accepting it. "It must have been so hard," they would naturally follow up. I nod because it is easier to accept their projections of me than to correct them. I try not to allow it to define me, but the consequences of it do.

For me, my father's rendition is not the most difficult part to accept. Many might assume that his physical displacement from our family affected us the most. But for me, the uncertainty of his location, the vagueness, the ambiguity around his wellbeing is what affected me long-term. Ironically, I love to travel. But when a loved one is away, I am constantly anxious. The fear of abandonment, of disappearance, the fear of having to battle the system as my mother did.

My husband's imprisonment caused much suffering, but it also gave me a better understanding of myself and the world. Between 2005 and 2015, the Harper government worked tirelessly to create an atmosphere of suspicion towards Muslims and division between different communities, raising some and lowering others. He introduced several antiterror bills, the most prominent one being Bill C-51, which became the antiterrorism law 2.0.

Under the pretext of protecting Canadians from Islamic terrorism, Harper and his government created a law that opened the door to the "criminalization" of dissent. From Muslims, the most obvious targets, the law crept to include Indigenous and environmental activists, and national security became so loose as to include "economic" interests as well.

When a community is targeted by an intrusive measure, few will oppose it, a few will cheer it, and many others will keep silent, as if they don't feel concerned or affected by it. Obviously, this is wrong. We have seen the damages that these intrusive and discriminatory laws had done to one community and gradually to others. Unfortunately, when the majority realizes the dangers of these laws, it would be too late to fight back.

The same argument can apply to the security certificates. First, many Canadians didn't feel concerned. They either ignored them or were not even aware of their existence. Some even accepted the argument that these measures were only intended for refugees and permanent residents. As if because of their status, refugees and permanent residents deserve fewer rights. Today, many of these secret measures are used against Canadians in Canadian courts. Discrimination is like a stone thrown in a calm lake. It makes ripples that become larger and larger.

Nineteen years ago, I was annoyed when journalists kept asking me what I was doing on 9/11. But the journalists also helped me train my memory, because I will never forget.

My therapist recently told me that regardless of a parent's intention, their absence, wilful or otherwise, marks you. It is simple child psychology. Someone I loved, someone who was supposed to love me, was missing. That is what registered in my mind. She added that every time I experience, witness, or even read about Islamophobia, I get retraumatized in some way. I had never thought about it that way, but I believe she is right. I am not the only one. All of the families whose fathers were ripped away must experience the same sentiments. There is often a lump in my throat or a knot in my stomach, afraid to hear of the next story targeting Muslims. Sometimes I stop reading the news as a coping mechanism. I feel that being a visibly Muslim woman and a writer, I should stay informed. I should have an opinion; I should claim my voice.

But it is a damned if you do, damned if you don't situation. If I remain silent, I am accused of being oppressed, uninformed, and uneducated. If I speak out, if I challenge the status quo, if I point the finger at what I believe is my real oppressor—neoliberalism—I am accused of being a mouthpiece for a male jihadist brainwashing me. Or, alternatively, I'll be told that if I don't like the West, I can see myself right out, much like Sunera Thobani was told after criticizing the American response to 9/11.

At a black-tie reception I attended instead of my mother earlier this year, my plus one—my roommate—asked me how I know so many politicians, university administrators, and artists. I told her, without a second thought, that it is because of my father's case. I was catapulted into spaces many Canadians would otherwise not have access to. I am told I act wiser than my age. Adults think it is a compliment, but it is a euphemism: I underwent much more trauma than most kids. I knew how to interact with adults because I had to learn. I was comfortable at vigils, protests, and even on Parliament Hill before the age of ten.

This is the first time I have written publicly about my father's affair. I understand what happened intellectually; I even read papers about my father's experience. I am sure that in some way, my academic work on violence and torture is related to my personal experiences as the daughter of someone who underwent that. But the newspapers and the journals all have a concise and sanitized version of events. And this is not an objective story. Trauma is never an objective story.

My father was collateral in the war on terror. And our family was collateral by proxy.

2001 | Mediating Thobani

Lynn Coady

Did you know that Sunera Thobani is "an idiot," "loathsome," "nutty," and "sick"? Maybe you didn't know this a week ago, but I bet you know it now.

How about this? Did you know that to be opposed to US foreign policy in general—or not to throw yourself body-and-soul behind the US government—is tantamount to showing your approval for the terrorist attacks on September 11? Did you know this means that you are attempting to justify the bombings? Did you know that this means you are a monster?

I bet you know it now—and, thanks to Sunera Thobani, I bet you'll think twice about articulating such heresy in the future.

I am not going to state the obvious and say that the terrorist attacks were a horrific tragedy. Not just because I shouldn't have to, but because, if I do, and then go on to make any kind of criticism of the prevailing spirit of war and retribution dominating popular opinion, then I am—if you believe the editorial staff of our national newspapers—essentially applauding the actions of terrorists.

It is a damn good thing that people like me have the pundits to keep us in line. They let us know that to even complete the statement, "The terrorist attacks were horrible and wrong, but . . ." is "despicable." I take this specific directive straight from the editorial desk of that bastion of free speech, the *Globe and Mail.*

Recently, on CBC radio's *This Morning*, Michael Enright hosted *New York Times* cultural critic Edward Rothstein. The latter delivered precisely the same message to Canadian listeners—that it is immoral even to contemplate finishing the above sentence. That "but" is the gateway to infamy, and Canadians are best advised to stay far, far away from it in thought and deed. Enright, admirably fighting off the journalistic impulse, certainly didn't deign to question or examine this formula for good citizenry.

The *Globe*'s Margaret Wente has big-heartedly suggested we should thank Sunera Thobani for, through the tenor of her speech, demonstrating how stupid and morally bankrupt feminists really are. The argument, parroted across the board by Wente's fellow pundits, goes something like this:

> Sunera Thobani says women are oppressed. However, Thobani was "permitted" (oh delicious irony: through the very democratic rights upheld by the nation she was criticizing!) to get up and speak her mind at a conference. Therefore, women are not oppressed. Therefore, Thobani is not oppressed and, if she hates North America so much (this is the *Vancouver Sun*'s Pete McMartin weighing in), why is she here, in the West she so apparently loathes?

Oh, but McMartin hastens to add, "This isn't a rhetorical 'Love It or Leave It' chest thump," but merely "an honest-to-goodness question." (Just like, say, "Why don't you go back where you came from?")

In one unified flourish, representatives of the Canadian media have leapt on the opportunity to discredit feminism, academic intellectuals, and academia in general. How many times has it been disdainfully pointed out this past week that the government gave $80,000 to the university conference where Thobani voiced her criticisms? That's $80,000, in case you didn't get it the first time, $80,000 of hard-earned taxpayers' money.

Most frightening, however, is the way in which Thobani's speech has been used to reinforce the appalling chill that has fallen over free speech in this country and the US. Over the past month, journalists and public figures who haven't fallen into line with the Wentes and McMartins of the world have been censored, reprimanded and, in some cases, fired for offering anything other than wholehearted support of the US government and whatever course of action George W. Bush deems fit to follow.

And yet, in their blithe, gleefully uninformed manner, pundits like Christie Blatchford claim that the opinions expressed by Sunera Thobani reflect the thinking of "those who actually run the country"—the "ruling elite."

Could it be that by "ruling elite," Blatchford is referring to the occasional letter writer to the *Globe* or the *National Post* or the *Vancouver Sun*? Otherwise, from what I can see, the "ruling elite" is very much united against thoughtful criticism, sociopolitical context, and thoroughgoing debate with regard to "America's New War."

In the past week, I have seen not one word of approval, or even sympathy, for Sunera Thobani in the editorial pages of our national media. I have heard not one word of support from any single politician—even those supposedly on the left.

Meanwhile, Thobani has found it necessary to post a security guard outside her office door—thanks, largely, to the fact that the local media has stopped just short of calling for her head. If there's a ruling elite that supports the opinions of Sunera Thobani, I can only assume they're in hiding.

And these days, you can't really blame them, now, can you?

Originally published on October 10, 2001.

2002 | Faces in the Crowd

Erin George

Activists of all stripes from across the country are dancing and chanting in the bright Calgary sun this week. Rabble spoke with protesters of the G8 Summit to find out why.

Pat Fritzel is a sixty-six-year-old farmer who describes herself as a granny who is raging. She drove to Calgary with six other members of the Salmon Arm chapter of the Council of Canadians:

> The governments are in the pockets of the corporations. I'm concerned about poverty in the Third World and in our own country. The G8 is all tied in together with the WTO [World Trade Organization] and NAFTA [North American Free Trade Agreement], which are eroding our rights. We're losing our health care. Education is being affected. And pensions are being threatened. Here in Calgary they've put up barricades as if we are really dangerous people, they are trying to stifle dissent. But as much as we can, we're going to make some noise.

Ursule Beaulieu is a sixty-one-year-old Catholic nun from Rimouski, Quebec. She is involved in her local women's centre and was in Quebec City for the demonstrations against the Free Trade Area of the Americas:

I'm here because I want justice and peace for everyone in the world. The G8 want globalization and it's not good for the people. In globalization, the poor are becoming so poor and the rich are becoming so rich. We want equity and liberty respected. For a lot of years now the G8 have said they will do something [about poverty] and they have not. So I'm not expecting that they will be better now because for all this time they have done nothing.

Loretta Gerlach is the Prairie Regional Organizer with the Council of Canadians. She travelled to Calgary with a contingent of Saskatchewan activists:

I think there are three reasons why people from Saskatchewan are here in Calgary. One of them is that we strongly believe in people before profits and the importance of showing our passion for the issues. Two, to show solidarity with our brothers and sisters in Alberta and show our dissent with them. And three, to add to the message that we are in this together. The agenda of the G8 affects people in Saskatchewan in many ways, the most notable would be through the WTO and the GATS [General Agreement on Trade in Services]. A number of our municipalities have passed resolutions asking to be exempt from the WTO and any trade agreements they would sign. And there are also the environmental implications such as water, hog barns, all those things. It's a big issue for Saskatchewan.

Roy Ward is a sixty-eight-year-old retiree. Ward endured a fifty-hour bus ride from Toronto to join the Calgary protests against the G8:

I want to leave this country in good shape for my children. These people who are running the government are not doing that. They're too incompetent and they're too greedy. They don't give two hoots about anything but themselves, money, and the corporate agenda. I want this country and this world given back to the people. It's been taken away. Globalization is going to kill us all and I'll fight until the end.

Meredith Bragg is a fifteen-year-old high school student. She marched with a contingent of Calgary Youth for Human Rights:

> I have a lot of problems with the G8. It's completely undemocratic how they've decided to come together. They've just decided that they are the most powerful nations and that they can run the entire world following their own rules. There's no transparency in their meetings – they have to tell people what's going on. Take Third World debt. It's disgusting that billons of people are living on less than $1(US) a day when there's these capitalist people with so much money. The distribution of wealth is disgusting. And the G8 is perpetuating that. The G8 pretends they're solving things but they're just making everything worse. The G8 pretends that they're cancelling Third World debt but they're not. They're making the debt payments worse and making countries even more in debt. It's horrible. I hope that as a group we can show people that what the G8 is doing is not okay, and there are people out there who disagree with them.

Hassan Yussuff is in Calgary with the Canadian Labour Congress (CLC):

> This is a continuation of the work that the CLC has been doing to resist corporate globalization and, of course, the hegemony they've had on the global agenda around development and around strategies for creating jobs. We were in Quebec City, in Windsor and in Seattle to send a message that if we are going to truly win in this broader struggle, we have to form broader coalitions. What these guys are really discussing, in terms of the African initiative, is really how to privatize and deregulate what little is left in Africa. In addition to that, the G8 want to say, "The only way you're going to win is to adopt the neoliberal agenda." It hasn't worked for twenty years, there's no reason why Africa should now trust that NEPAD [the New Partnership for African Development] is going to give them what they are looking for to create jobs, to develop their economy and to provide health care and education for the people. While they're fighting to regain

> some sense of direction for how to develop in Africa, we're fighting to maintain what we have won in the past. If we can't link our hands with African brothers and sisters in this global struggle, we're never going to make any headway in the broader struggle that we are fighting: corporate globalization and capitalism.

Selam Michael is a thirty-two-year-old Eritrean-born Canadian. She came to the Calgary protests to add her voice to the call for an Africa for Africans, not for the G8:

> I'm from East Africa and the country is Eritrea. It is a country that does not abide by the rules of the IMF [International Monetary Fund] or World Bank. We decide what to do with our lives, with our nation. I don't like the agenda of the G8 and I know that they have been creating a lot of problems in Third World countries. Especially because I am from a Third World country, I should be here [in protest]. They always want to portray Africa as a continent of people who are desperate and poor and starving. We are also fighting back. But there is a reason why we are so poor and desperate and hungry, and that's because someone has taken advantage of the resources and wealth. So I want these people to hear a different voice. I'm here to add my voice to the struggle.

Virginia Setshedi travelled from Soweto, Johannesburg, to speak out against NEPAD at the Group of Six Billion (G6B) People's Summit; an active member of the Soweto Electricity Crisis Committee, she is leading the fight against power privatization in South Africa:

> One of the things I see in NEPAD is that it is continuously promoting the neoliberal agenda and the interests of the corporations while shelving the interests and needs of the poor and working class of all of Africa. It might be called new, but NEPAD is nothing new. It's full of old tricks, old strategies and old processes that have failed and led us into a situation where we don't have electricity, water, health facilities and where we have high rates of disease like HIV/AIDS. Instead of

coming together with civil society to sit down and decide what's best for the whole of the continent, our presidents are meeting behind closed doors and taking decisions on our behalf that are going to affect us for the rest of our lives. That's why as part of civil society, especially in Africa, we say "down with NEPAD, down!"

Lorie Peacock is a member of the Canadian Auto Workers' local 199 in St. Catharines, Ontario. She and other workers came to Calgary to bring the movement home:

> We feel it's important to take the information [we learn here] not only back to our membership but also back to our community. So we're going to get a cross section of people who are here in Calgary representing labour, health, the environment, and education and put on a forum back at our union hall in St. Catharines. That way people can see, first and foremost, that we're not a bunch of radicals here to smash buildings, drink beer, or cause destruction and trouble. We're here for a reason. We believe that as workers and as communities, things can be better for us. And that those eight people who are making the decisions are not making the decisions on behalf of the six billion of us. They're making decisions on behalf of corporations. There are many ways of participating [in this movement] that aren't necessarily the big ones. Everyone can do their own little part and that's just as important as being here in Calgary protesting the G8.

Christina Stebanuk is a member of the Calgary Disability Action Hall. She brought her five-year-old son to the march. She's here to show the link between the poverty that people with disabilities face and the G8 agenda:

> We're in solidarity with this march because we [people with disabilities] live in poverty as well. If they go ahead with the G8 agenda, we will continue to be in poverty. We're here to support the march and to give our solidarity. One example is that the bus passes in Calgary are going up to $60 and we only have a limited income of $855 [a month];

so if they keep raising the bus passes we're not going to be able to come out to events like this.

Suzanne Quinsey is a nurse at a Toronto hospital. She also volunteers as a street nurse providing health care for the homeless:

The G8 and the control they have takes away from what a democracy should be. I want to protest this style of government where the average person isn't in control. These issues come up in health care. Even if we wanted a better health care system, the government is so connected to the health care industry it's disgusting what they are doing and how that's changing our health care system. It's deteriorated to such a degree that I basically don't want to work at a hospital anymore. To reduce costs, the hospital I work in has contracted out lab services and security. That deteriorates working conditions and increases workload.

Originally published in a three-part series, June 25–27, 2002.

2003 | September 11, 1973

Carlos A. Torres

On September 11, 1973, the presidential palace of La Moneda in Santiago, Chile, was attacked by warplanes, and the democratically elected president, Salvador Allende, was killed. This military coup marked the first day of the seventeen-year dictatorial regime of Augusto Pinochet, years marked with terror and bloodshed for thousands of Chileans. Between 1973 and 1990, Chileans endured arbitrary detention, torture, disappearances, killings, and exile.

On the morning of Tuesday, September 11, 2001, I was once again overwhelmed with feelings of grief and loss. From that day on, September 11 will also carry painful memories for most citizens of the United States. As I watched the terror unfold in New York and Washington, it was difficult for me to comprehend the possibility of it all, but it also triggered images in my mind that changed my life for good on that same day twenty-eight years before.

Television images showing planes flying into the World Trade Center were horrific reminders of the warplanes that bombed Chile's government palace. The search for survivors and the rising death toll were reminders of my own loved ones lost. Many of their bodies, thirty years later, have still not been found. Relatives of the victims carrying placards with names and photographs of their loved ones created a cruel parallel. In Chile and other countries of the Americas, these images have become sadly familiar over the past decades.

In my stunned silence, I recognized the common denominator in these two tragedies—both were terrorist attacks on civilians and innocent people. One difference lies in the fact that while the American people were victims of individual terrorism, the Chileans were victims of state terrorism. Clearly, it is difficult to draw symmetry between the two countries, yet one more commonality exists. In both abominable cases, the United States was part of the equation. In 2001 it was the victim, but sadly, on that very same date back in 1973, it was the perpetrator.

Even before President Salvador Allende was elected, the US Secretary of State at the time, Henry Kissinger, approved the funding, weaponry, and logistical support necessary to topple the Chilean democratic system. Later, when the attempt to stop the Chilean Congress from ratifying the newly elected president failed, the Secretary of State, along with the Forty Committee, orchestrated an economic boycott and political campaign to overthrow Allende through a coup d'état. These operations took place for almost four years until the Allende government was ultimately crushed.

In preparation for and during the coup d'état, military personnel of the Chilean armed forces were trained by the United States School of the Americas, completing courses specializing in the annihilation of political dissidents, leftists, progressive organizations, and labour unions. The curriculum of the School of the Americas included procedures of physical and psychological torture, terrorist attacks, rape, control, and murder. This military school, which previously operated in the Panama Canal Zone, is still open for business today in Fort Benning, Georgia. Terrorist gangs were also financed and trained by the CIA and the US government to kidnap and kill, a fact recently revealed by the international press.

As innocent people in the United States still recover from a terrible tragedy and the unbearable pain it caused, it has become more important than ever to discuss the responsibility of its subsequent governments and state agencies in the promotion and endorsement of terrorist activities. The people of Chile have endured this kind of pain for many years.

Chileans in exile have mourned the loss of life, loss of country, loss of identity and loss of a dream for the past three decades, while within Chile, the wounds created by the coup d'état are still very much open.

In my own mourning, additional parallels form questions in my mind.

In Canada, after September 11, 2001, we declared a day of mourning for the victims of the terrorist attacks in the US as a symbolic tribute to the many lives taken and the pain endured. Why was it not as appropriate to do something similar when the Rwanda massacre occurred in 1994? Or following the many other horrible tragedies our world has endured? It seems that there is a grotesque and calculated lack of balance in the compassion shown for victims of violence and terror—that a powerful nation can mourn and retaliate in the name of its citizens while an impoverished nation can only lament casualties imposed on them.

Respect for justice and observation of international treaties and human rights can be a legitimate and powerful response to terrorism—to terrorist acts conducted by states and their agencies as well as those masterminded by individuals and fundamentalist groups of any rank. Most agree that anyone involved in human rights violations, torture, and terrorist attacks should be taken to justice. So should this not also be the case for Ariel Sharon—for his participation in the massacres at Sabra and Shatilla? Or for Henry Kissinger and other US government officials involved in terrorist actions in Latin America for the past thirty years? President George W. Bush's war against terrorism ought to include state-sponsored terrorism, and he should be willing to open up cases that have been covered up so tightly as to prevent real answers for millions of citizens in the Americas whose lives have been destroyed.

In the same way, all individuals involved in terrorist activities against sovereign states and nations should be tried. US agencies implicated in financing and sponsoring plots against other countries and leaders who disagree with US government policies should be made accountable and eventually dismantled. The names of foreign political leaders and officers who receive bribes from the White House and the CIA should be revealed to face justice in their own countries for treason. If President Bush is earnest in his commitment to democratic values, he must do this.

In October of 1970, three years before the coup d'état in Chile, the

Richard Nixon administration via Henry Kissinger authorized the kidnapping and assassination of the commander-in-chief of the Chilean army, General Rene Schneider. On October 22, he was murdered. The weapons, money, and further support to plotters were provided by US State agencies. Later, Nixon and Kissinger, along with ITT, Pepsi Cola, Chase Manhattan, and the CIA, took necessary actions and allocated millions of dollars to "make the Chilean economy scream"—in the words of Richard Helms, then director of the CIA.

According to archived notes, Helms, David Rockefeller of Chase Manhattan, and Donald Kendall of Pepsi Cola were present at meetings where the destabilization of the Allende government was planned. The intention was to create conditions for a military coup through terrorist activity, assassination, and economic boycotts. The impact of open US intervention in Chile did not fade with time; after the coup, the US provided more support and diplomatic aid to the dictatorial regime. In the case of the attacks against the US, we hope the situation will be different—that the effects on society will finally fade, and people will find much-needed peace.

In Chile today, some of the military individuals responsible for brutal human rights violations are facing jail terms. However, the terror-mongers are still at large. The Chilean elite and their US supporters are enjoying the benefits of the system they helped put in place through violence and terror. The former have built a political system and economic model that solely protects their greedy interests, while the latter enjoy the power provided by their military might.

Today, thirty years after the coup d'état, Chileans have renewed hopes in their search for truth, justice, and democracy, which includes full disclosure of US intervention in the internal affairs of a sovereign state. In the US, the relatives and friends of the September 11, 2001 victims still wait for full exposure of the tragic events that have altered their lives. We hope that the US government will change its course and become a beacon of justice, democracy, and truth. If this happens, then maybe peace will prevail one day for US citizens and people of the world. Otherwise, we are sure to be exposed to more tragedy and terrorism. The US government might have lost this opportunity two years ago by attacking and blindly retaliating against unclear suspects and obliterating vast communities in Afghanistan. Perhaps history will help us to reverse a wasted opportunity that will allow us to build peace instead of fostering war and aggression.

Certainly, the invasion of Iraq does not help curtail terrorism or achieve peace in an already disarrayed world. These attacks can only unleash more terrorism, instability, and hate as we have witnessed in Iraq. Once again, the connection between the Iraqi government and terrorist networks has not been proven, nor has the existence of weapons of mass destruction. However, thousands of lives have been destroyed in the name of peace and preventing wars. The very idea of preventing conflict began a long time ago, the Chilean case an example, where intervention followed the Nixon-Kissinger logic that Chileans must be prevented from "going Marxist."

After all these tragedies and many others, the US government still makes no apologies. Paradoxically, my anger against the government of the United States and its previous administration for the events of September 11, 1973, in Chile is coupled with great sympathy and regret for its innocent citizens who tragically died on the same date in 2001.

Originally published on September 11, 2003.

2004 Appeasement: Selling Out on Missile

Duncan Cameron

Appeasement is one of the most important words of the twentieth century. Winston Churchill was the famous opponent of this policy of conciliation, which can also be thought of as a willingness to sell out others in order to gain peace for oneself.

When the UK government tried to appease Hitler at Munich by handing over a part of Czechoslovakia, Churchill roared that the dictator would come back for more now that his appetite had been whetted, since the policy of Germany was mastery of Europe.

Under Mackenzie King, the Liberals supported appeasement. It was widely thought the Treaty of Versailles, which ended World War I, was unjust and that Germany's legitimate grievances should be met. This explains the support in Canada (and elsewhere) for the appeasement policy until Munich.

Churchill's triumph—he was right, his opponents wrong; they adopted his policies and invited him to lead them in a new direction—inspired American leaders to label as appeasers those who opposed the war in Vietnam.

The inaccuracy of the historical analogy was obvious: communism was not fascism, Ho Chi Minh was not Hitler, the Indochina peninsula was not Europe, and the struggle for national liberation was not an attempt to conquer and enslave other nations.

While the Americans lost the Vietnam War, their appetite for Churchill-like victories remains. The years since the world saw American soldiers evacuate Saigon have amounted to a thirty-year-war to maintain American economic and political preeminence. The fall of the Berlin Wall and the break-up of the Soviet Union have changed little in the world of US policy-makers. The pursuit of world military supremacy continues.

Mel Hurtig's new book *Rushing to Armageddon* shows the new insecurity arising from the American plan to deploy a so-called missile defence system. Other great powers, notably Russia and China, are signalling their intent to follow suit and renew their nuclear arsenals. The folly of missile defence leads to a continued misallocation of world resources badly needed for eradication of disease and meeting basic needs.

As announced in interviews given by its defence minister, the Paul Martin government policy on missile defence is apologetic. It will cost Canada nothing to participate, there are no plans to deploy US interceptor missiles on our territory, we will benefit from the enhanced defence capability, and since the Americans are going ahead anyway, we gain nothing by opposing missile defence. This is the government line.

In a word, the Liberal policy towards the United States is appeasement.

If Paul Martin were a real world leader, he would give a speech at Yale University laying out the dangers to world peace of the American missile defence scheme. His speechwriters could choose from various irrefutable arguments and winning themes. Missile defence is understood as enhanced first strike capacity by other great powers, thus threatening deterrence. The domestic benefits for the US of de-escalation of the arms build-up are great; mortgaging national credit to put missiles in space imposes steep costs in lost opportunities for education, housing, transport, etc.

Expect nothing of the sort to come out of Ottawa. Another way of defining appeasement is as a bribe. By making concessions to American policy, which is driven by the desire to increase military domination, and sacrificing principles of multilateral co-operation to build common security, the policy supported by the Canadian public, the Martin government wants something in return.

What is it that is driving Liberal appeasement? Only this: to be pardoned for not providing troops to Iraq and be excused for wanting cross-border trade (often between American corporations on either side of the border) to go ahead without security concerns closing the Ambassador Bridge to, say, General Motors products. No wonder that the next Canadian ambassador to Washington is rumoured to be the head of the Canadian Council of Chief Executives, Tom d'Aquino.

The issues raised by missile defence go to the heart of what makes a world dominated by great power politics unacceptable. The legitimate concerns of the world are ignored while the hegemonic power follows its own blueprint.

Canadian support for missile defence represents an abdication of our role as an independent country with a role to play in the world. Canada stands for international co-operation through the UN, or it supports American unilateralism; it acts in concert with others who oppose the project, or it adopts the role of lackey.

Is there anyone who seriously believes that Canadian support for this project will advance world peace? No. Nor will it improve Canada's standing in Washington. The next time the Americans want something from us, our participation will gain us no leverage, and when we want their support, our nonparticipation will lose us no advantage.

Originally published on October 6, 2004.

2005 | One Thousand and One Nights

Maha Zimmo

On September 6, 2005, it will have been 1,001 nights since Sophie Harkat's husband Mohamed was arrested via the Canadian Security Intelligence Service (CSIS) Certificate, accused of having ties to terrorists. Justified as protecting "us" from "them," the security certificates are used against permanent residents or refugees as a means to detain and, potentially, deport them.

Alf Layla wa Layla, more commonly known as "One Thousand and One Nights," is one of the most famous Middle Eastern stories known to the Western world. The heroine, Scheherazade, survives her nights by spinning a multitude of tales encompassing the macabre, the violent, the sexual, and the mystical to a spellbound Caliph. During the course of our evening, Sophie became my personal Scheherazade.

Like Scheherazade, Sophie also fights for her own survival. An assault on a lover is an assault on one's self; the deportation and its almost certain consequence—the torture of Mohamed—would claim a mirrored casualty in the heart of Sophie.

Mohamed is one of the "Secret Trial Five": men of Arab Muslim background, detained without charge, threatened with deportation to countries from which they fled. "Evidence" against them is presented at secret trials, "secret" for national security reasons. Both the accused and their lawyers are barred from the trials and from identifying and cross-examining witnesses, allowed access only to minimal summarized "evidence." The decision rendered by the federal judge cannot be appealed.

This tale that could easily be yours or mine is of a Canadian girl who fell in love with and married the "wrong" man at the "wrong moment in time"—a Muslim Arab man in a post-9/11 world.

Sophie tells how, after a banal blind date, she walked into a gas station on St-Joseph Boulevard in Ottawa. She animatedly illustrates what she must have looked like while the stranger behind the counter was attempting to engage her in conversation as she was buried in the refrigerator, rummaging for Diet Pepsi. Not being in the mood to speak with "some guy," she explains how she "looked up and he had these big brown eyes and very beautiful long lashes. He smiled at me and lifted me up."

After eight months of many Diet Pepsis, Moe finally asked Sophie on their first date. Sophie, not one to mince words, exploded with an incensed, "He's not my type at all. He's short. Tiny! I found out only after I started liking him! He is the sweetest person I know. I love how he laughs like a child. I went from 'he's not my type' to now finding only men who look like him attractive! Imagine?" I nodded because I believe in the Arabic word *naseeb*, which, loosely translated, means "fate," but a fate that pertains to only a few instances in our lives, one of them being the moment we meet our partners.

Married on January 2, 2001, their first year and a half of marriage was troubled by Moe's gambling addiction and their conflicting schedules. He was working three jobs; Sophie would occasionally warn that he might one day come home to find his suitcases packed. This was of course an empty threat. "I never did this. I love him too much."

By October 2002, Moe had barred himself from the casino in an effort to change his life. Two months later, on the day of his arrest, all of Moe's endeavours would be paralyzed.

Since the arrest, Sophie has suffered from high blood pressure, migraines, and irregular heartbeat. Having difficulty sleeping, she is forced to nap in the afternoons to avoid "crashing" later in the day. Glaucoma has set in, and occasionally, her back "locks," and she is left in severe pain. Her diabetes has worsened, requiring her to take higher doses of medication. Her doctors concur that Sophie suffers the physical manifestations of intolerable stress. In the absence of guilt, how will the Canadian government quantify and make amends for this reality?

Though quantifying physical pain can make the wreckage of the security certificates more tangible, it is nearly impossible to do the same with emotion. As with the physical trauma, will the government be held accountable for the emotional pain? Looking to understand this consequence, I ask Sophie pointed questions but receive surface responses about "anger."

Angry at: some of her family's remaining doubt as to Mohamed's innocence (on occasion, they mutter "Well, you married a Muslim"); the government that robbed her of her husband; her fellow Canadians who know and don't care, and those who don't care to know. Angry that she has been forced to take nearly two years of medical leave without pay and angry that, should she not return to work in October 2005, she will become unemployed.

Angry that she is forced to speak to her husband through Plexiglass, only touching him twice in the course of the last thirty-one months, both times while in court and in public.

Finally, Sophie admits, "I miss his laugh. Simple things. I miss his smell. Washing his clothes, and arguing. I even miss stupid things, like him making me watch things on television I hate." After a pause, she adds, "Now I watch them alone, even though I still think they're stupid."

"Knowing the full social, physical and emotional consequences of loving Moe, would you do it again?" Unflinchingly, Sophie responds with "yes."

Whereas we know Scheherazade's fate, Sophie possesses no such foresight into her future. She expresses fear, worrying that such severe and prolonged separation may leave emptiness between her and Moe. The language that is shared by lovers, in this case spanning religions and cultures, existing beyond the physical and only understood by them is hard to sustain under the most normal conditions. Undeniably, Sophie's fears are valid.

My final question to Sophie is the hardest to pose since these security certificates permit indefinite detention. Does she want to have children with Moe? Her response is unusual for this self-proclaimed "open book who'll tell you anything." Avoiding my eyes, Sophie sidesteps the subject.

I let her catch her breath and then ask the question again. Eyes wide, she peeks out at me from behind her glasses, smiles and answers, "Yes. I just want to see what [the baby] will look like." Though I laughed at the absurdity of her response, I was sobered by the thought that she and Moe may never have this luxury, my heart breaking for the men detained, their families, and our Canada.

Originally published on August 26, 2005.

2006–2010 | Section 2: Anti/reconciliation in Canada

Self-Determination or Re-Colonization? Stephen Harper and the Indian Act

Russell Diabo

From the Confederation era to the present, the Indian Act has been the foundation for Canada's colonization of Indigenous peoples. Despite numerous amendments since its adoption in 1876, the Indian Act of today maintains the tenets of protection, control, and "civilization"—meaning assimilation. It was the Indian Act that provided the legal and political impetus for the residential school system, and it is the Indian Act that continues to erode Indigenous communities across the country today.

In 1969, about a century after the Indian Act became law, Prime Minister Pierre Elliot Trudeau and his then Minister of Indian Affairs, Jean Chrétien, argued that poverty in Indigenous communities was a result of discriminatory laws, and that the equal treatment of Indigenous people was the solution. The Trudeau government published a white paper that outlined a series of policy recommendations that centred on the elimination of "Indian" as a distinct legal status. The white paper also suggested, among other things, that Canada eliminate the Department of Indian Affairs, convert reserve land into private property, eventually terminate treaties, and abolish the Indian Act. Indigenous peoples and organizations across Canada fiercely opposed these proposals, which represented an attempt to assimilate Indigenous peoples and shirk responsibility for upholding Aboriginal and treaty rights. The opposition eventually forced the federal government to withdraw the white paper in 1971.

However, internal correspondence shows that terminating collective Aboriginal and treaty rights has remained the federal objective ever since. In 1970, a deputy minister at the Department of Indian Affairs, David A. Munro, wrote a letter to another deputy minister, urging him not to abandon the white paper plan, but to instead simply change tactics: "We need not change the policy content, but we should put varying degrees of emphasis on its several components and we should try to discuss it in terms of its components rather than as a whole," wrote Munro.

A year later, Chrétien wrote to Trudeau confirming that the goals elucidated in the white paper lived on:

> We are deliberately furthering an evolutionary process of provincial and Indian inter-involvement by promoting contacts at every opportunity at all levels of government, at the same time recognizing the truth of the matter – that progress will take place in different areas in different ways at a different pace. Experience shows that the reference of a time frame in the policy paper of 1969 was one of the prime targets of those who voiced the Indian opposition to the proposals. *The course upon which we are now embarked seems to present a more promising approach to the long-term objectives than might be obtained by setting specific deadlines for relinquishing federal administration.* (emphasis added)

While the federal government had publicly rescinded the white paper, the bureaucracy quietly continued to implement it, policy by policy, and over a longer timeframe.

The legal situation changed in 1982, as First Nations pushed for the recognition of Aboriginal and treaty rights in section 35 of Canada's new constitution. During negotiations, representatives of First Nations and Canada's first ministers failed to reach an agreement on the meaning of Aboriginal and treaty rights. This failure to reach constitutional consensus has created legal—and political—uncertainty about the constitutional definition of Aboriginal and treaty rights of First Nations, making it possible for successive federal governments to continue attempts to extinguish Indigenous rights despite their recognition in the constitution.

My contention is that the overall federal objective is to coerce First Nations into signing agreements with the government (called Self-government/Comprehensive Land Claims Agreements) that will compromise their Aboriginal and treaty rights for "new" significantly reduced rights and a few token "benefits" in the form of converting reserves into private property land and some cash.

Federal governments, whether Liberal or Conservative, have coerced First Nations' consent, band by band, group by group, to surrender First Nations preexisting sovereignty in order to accept the assertion of Crown sovereignty over—as section 91.24 of the Constitution Act 1867 puts it—"Indians and Lands reserved for the Indians," which contributes to the federal objective of emptying section 35 of Canada's new 1982 constitution of any real or significant meaning. As I write this, approximately thirty Indigenous groups in Canada have already compromised their section 35 rights by signing on to Comprehensive Land Claims Agreements or Self-Government Agreements. Still more Indigenous groups are at negotiating tables today.

Canada intensifies its "war" on a First Nation when a First Nation resists and tries to assert Aboriginal or treaty rights over lands and resources beyond what the federal government will allow. It is vital to understand the period from 2006 through 2010, Stephen Harper's first mandate, within this context.

Pre-Harper Kelowna Accord

In November 2005, just before the Harper government came to power, then-Prime Minister Paul Martin held a First Ministers' Meeting (FMM) in Kelowna, BC, to discuss Aboriginal issues. The Kelowna meeting, like other occasions when federal leaders deem it useful and expedient, invited national Indigenous political advocacy organizations—the Assembly of First Nations, the Inuit Tapiriit Kanatami, and the Métis National Council—to participate in a federal, top-down consultation process. The

Assembly of First Nations (AFN) is a political advocacy body for the chiefs across Canada. It is not a people's organization, it is a chief's organization—and only chiefs recognized under the Indian Act can be AFN delegates.

First Nations communities were not included in the top-down process, and local Indigenous activists who opposed the meeting organized a demonstration outside of the hotel where the meeting was taking place.

The meeting in Kelowna only dealt with the symptoms of First Nations and other Indigenous people's poverty, not the causes. Without the political will to address these root causes—namely, lands and resources taken without proper compensation or consent, a lack of respect for Aboriginal and treaty rights, and a failure to recognize First Nations' right to self-determination—the meeting in Kelowna didn't lead to any substantive changes. Instead, the meeting focused on the escalating costs of delivering programs and services to First Nations (and other Aboriginal peoples) and debating which level of government should pay.

In the end, the only outcome of the meeting was a joint press release from the prime minister, premiers, and territorial leaders, which the media dubbed the "Kelowna Accord," and which the Harper government promptly buried after his election in 2006.

Residential Schools

In May 2006, the federal government signed an agreement with survivors of the residential school system. The Indian Residential School Settlement Agreement—co-signed by the churches, the AFN, and other Indigenous organizations—was intended to bring a fair, lasting resolution to the legacy of residential schools.

The agreement mandated five elements aimed at addressing the legacy of Indian Residential Schools, including the establishment of a Truth and Reconciliation Commission (TRC), and, crucially, an apology, which would come two years later. On June 11, 2008, Harper issued a scripted apology to residential school survivors with sincerity and, uncharacteristically for him, with humility.

At the time, Prime Minister Harper received much public support for his government's apology, including from AFN National Chief Phil Fontaine, who heralded the federal apology as a "new relationship" between First Nations and the federal government.

Of course, Harper's apology did not come from a spontaneous desire to express guilt on the part of the government or make amends with First Nations. Rather, it was mandated by the settlement agreement. And in the years leading up to his apology, the federal government faced significant pressure from class action lawsuits launched by residential school survivors from across Canada. Fearing the government might be held liable for a far larger amount of money than what was being negotiated under the settlement agreement, Harper settled with the AFN and the class action litigants. The resulting agreement required that a majority of the residential school survivors in the various class action lawsuits accept the terms of the negotiated IRS Settlement Agreement.

While many elderly survivors opted to accept the lesser amount offered under the IRS Settlement Agreement rather than wait for a lengthy judicial process to conclude, a significant number of survivors did not accept. Many of these individuals were survivors of severe physical or sexual abuse and remained openly hostile to National Chief Fontaine and the IRS Settlement Agreement, which used a highly invasive process to assess claims of physical or sexual abuse.

The IRS Settlement Agreement also mandated the establishment of a Truth and Reconciliation Commission (TRC). The TRC's main purpose was to put the residential school system into Canada's past and build a future in Canada based upon reconciliation, which the Supreme Court of Canada has ruled is the main purpose of section 35 of Canada's constitution.

But the TRC's mandate was limited. The TRC was not in itself a legal process, which distinguished it from truth commissions in other countries dealing with legacies of violence. TRC commissioners were not authorized to hold formal hearings, did not have the power to compel people to attend or participate in any of its events or activities, and could not name any individual responsible for abuses under the residential school system unless the person was already identified in a criminal court proceeding.

The TRC depended on voluntary participation and statements by those priests, nuns, church staff, and federal bureaucrats, many of whom were, at that time, still alive and culpable for the abuses carried out against former students in the Crown's name.

Moreover, neither Harper's apology nor the TRC addressed the Crown's real agenda during this period.

Abandoned Models of Self-Government

This isn't to say that efforts to decolonize from the Indian Act haven't been tried before. In 1983, when the constitution was shiny and new, a parliamentary committee was tasked with studying self-government. The Special Parliamentary Committee on Indian Self-Government comprised ex officio members from three national Indigenous organizations, the AFN, the Native Women's Association of Canada, and the Native Council of Canada. The committee held hearings across Canada and put forth a series of recommendations that became known as the Penner Report.

The committee recommended that "the federal government recognize First Nations as a distinct order of government within the Canadian federation and pursue processes leading to self-government."

The report proposed constitutional entrenchment of self-government and, in the short-term, the introduction of legislation to facilitate it. Unfortunately, a federal election was called shortly after the report's release in 1984, and the committee's recommendations were buried.

It wasn't until the early 1990s, when the federal government launched the Royal Commission on Aboriginal Peoples, that the issue of self-government was raised again. This commission's report recognized that "Aboriginal governments" have jurisdiction over "core areas" of responsibility, or in other words, a degree of "internal sovereignty." While the report's authors conducted a thorough analysis of the Indian Act, its recommendations, like those of the 1983 Penner Report, have largely been ignored by the federal politicians and bureaucrats to this day.

Instead of recognizing and affirming First Nations as a "distinct order of government" in Canada, both the Harper government and the Liberal government that would follow pursued a policy approach under which First Nations will eventually become ethnic municipalities.

Canada is not waging a conventional war against First Nations, and it is not covert, although there is a sophisticated propaganda machine in Ottawa that generates Crown public spin against First Nation interests in any dispute. The Crown war is essentially a legal-political-fiscal conflict over the interpretation, assertion, and implementation of Aboriginal and treaty rights over lands and resources by First Nations.

The Indian Act is still used as the primary statute of control and management from the federal constitutional power over "Indians and Lands reserved for the Indians," along with the coercive federal-provincial fiscal arrangements.

So when Prime Minister Harper said in 2008, "today, we recognize that this policy of assimilation was wrong, has caused great harm, and has no place in our country," he was only referring to the (by then) historic residential school system. He wasn't referring to the government's broader program of assimilation, which his government continued to carry out throughout the TRC process.

Canada's policy of pursuing self-government and land claims agreements with First Nations is designed to achieve the surrender of First Nations' preexisting sovereignty and territory, and to replace it with First Nations' acceptance of Crown sovereignty over "Indians and Lands reserved for the Indians" along with the federal definition and interpretation of section 35 "Aboriginal and Treaty" rights. In other words, the federal government's broad policy goal has been assimilation and the termination of preexisting collective rights.

UNDRIP and Hot Spots

More evidence of this assimilation-termination approach can be seen in the Harper government's response to the United Nations Declaration on the Rights of Indigenous Peoples (UNDRIP). In September 2007, the UN General Assembly approved the declaration. Four countries abstained: Australia, New Zealand, the United States, and Canada.

What do these four states have in common? They are all former British colonies with Indigenous peoples still living within them.

At the time, John McNee, Canada's ambassador to the UN, told the General Assembly, "The provisions in the declaration on lands, territories and resources are overly broad, unclear, and capable of a wide variety of interpretations." The federal minister of Indian affairs, Chuck Strahl, told the media, "The declaration is worded in such a way that it is inconsistent with the Canadian Constitution, the Charter, several acts of Parliament and existing treaties."

Reportedly, Prime Minister Harper had expressed concern about the language in the UN Declaration. Publicly, Harper said, "We shouldn't vote for things on the basis of political correctness; we should actually vote on the basis of what's in the document."

It wasn't until 2010 that the Canadian government announced its endorsement of UNDRIP. Why the change of policy? Quite likely it was because of electoral politics in the face of a looming federal election after a census showed a growing Indigenous population in key ridings.

John Duncan, then Minister of Aboriginal Affairs, said Canada had decided to officially endorse UNDRIP to "further reconcile and strengthen our relationship with Aboriginal peoples in Canada."

While the Harper government publicly endorsed UNDRIP, it claimed that the Declaration was merely an "aspirational" instrument and did not reflect customary international law. Under Harper, the federal government claimed, "the Declaration does not change Canadian laws. It represents an expression of political, not legal, commitment. Canadian laws define the bounds of Canada's engagement with the Declaration."

Although UNDRIP is not legally binding, it does contain minimum international standards for the human rights and treatment of Indigenous peoples. As Article 43 of the Declaration provides, the Articles "constitute the minimum standards for the survival, dignity and well-being of the indigenous peoples of the world."

In addition to UNDRIP, there are other legally binding documents that Canada is a signatory to, specifically the UN Covenant on Civil and Political Rights, the UN Covenant on Educational, Social and Cultural Rights, and the International Convention on the Elimination of Racial

Discrimination. Taken together, these three documents form the basis for the right of Indigenous peoples of self-determination in international law.

At the same time that Harper's government equivocated on UNDRIP, it was also spying on First Nations. Internal documents from Indian Affairs and the RCMP show that shortly after forming government in January 2006, Harper ordered the federal government to tighten up its gathering and sharing of intelligence on First Nations to anticipate and manage potential unrest in Indigenous communities against planned resource extraction projects across Canada.

Material obtained by Access to Information requests revealed that almost immediately upon taking power in 2006, the Department of Indian and Northern Affairs Canada (INAC) was given the lead role to spy on First Nations. The goal was to identify First Nation leaders, participants, and supporters of occupations and protests and closely monitor their actions.

To accomplish this task, INAC identified "hot spots"—those First Nations that were of "growing concern" due to "unrest" and increasing "militancy." They included bands from the coast of Vancouver Island to the shores of the Atlantic Ocean. Some of the "hot spot" communities included Caledonia, Ontario, where the Six Nations of the Grand River were resisting the development of a subdivision on their land; Belleville, Ontario, where allies were staging road blockades in solidarity with the Six Nations; Brantford, Ontario (Grand River Conservation Authority Lands); Deseronto, Ontario, where protesters occupied a quarry to protest subdivision development on unceded Tyendinaga land; and Grassy Narrows, Ontario, where environmental activists blockaded the Trans Canada Highway to protest logging on Grassy Narrows First Nation land.

One of these "hot spots" was the Algonquins of Barriere Lake, a community of about five hundred people, located in Quebec, just a three-hour drive north of Ottawa. For centuries, this community governed itself through a customary leadership system that managed their traditional territory, along with the other Algonquin communities in the Algonquin Nation, which straddles the Ottawa River in what are now the provinces of Quebec and Ontario.

In 1991, refusing to extinguish their Aboriginal title through the federal government's land claims policy, the Barriere Lake Algonquins pressed the federal and Quebec governments to sign a trilateral agreement that would create a research and planning process to prepare a sustainable development plan for forests and wildlife over their traditional territory.

The Algonquins wanted a process to address the massive clear-cutting taking place on their lands and the building of logging roads that opened up access to their territory to sports hunters and fishers. These logging activities destroyed wildlife habitat and created competition for fish and game without Algonquin consent, which impacted the community's ability to put food on the table as the Algonquins continue to rely on hunting, fishing, trapping and gathering for their sustenance.

Although the governments signed the agreement, both the federal and Quebec governments tried to get out of implementing it. In response, the Algonquins erected logging blockades and shut down the forestry industry in the region. The Algonquins also did traffic slow-downs and, on occasion, set up blockades on Highway 117, the only road for hundreds of kilometres that connected Quebec's northwest region to the south.

In response, the governments of Canada and Quebec intervened in Algonquin internal affairs and attempted to replace the customary chief, Jean Maurice Matchewan. Factions formed, and Matchewan was ultimately pressured to step down. He was replaced with an elder and former customary chief Harry Wawatie, who eventually also stepped down after the federal government put the community into "third party management"—essentially taking over the Algonquins' financial administration and putting the community under the control and management of the Department of Indian Affairs.

In 2010, applying a rarely used section of the Indian Act, section 74, the Harper government forced the Algonquins of Barriere Lake—one of the last pure custom bands in Canada—to hold elections under an electoral officer appointed by the federal government, and thus into the Indian Act elective system. (This was the same section of the act used in 1924 to force the Six Nations of the Grand River into an Indian Act election system.) Thus, the colonial Indian Act was used once again to replace an Indigenous community's traditional governance system with an elective system controlled by Ottawa and designed to force compliance with Ottawa's whims.

In the end, after thirty years of work on a sustainable development plan under the 1991 agreement, the divisions in the community sowed by the federal and Quebec governments resulted in the Barriere Lake community rejecting a proposal for the joint management of forests and wildlife on their traditional territory with the Quebec government. Now the Algonquins are back to where they were in the early 1990s, negatively impacted by provincial law, except now the community is also under the federal Indian Act elective system, not their own traditional government.

The Barriere Lake community was just one of the "hot spots" that Harper's government spied on during this period. Each week, federal officials prepared a "hot spot binder" with reports from the government's monitoring of Indigenous communities across the country who engaged in direct action to protect their lands.

Of particular concern to the federal government were "unpredictable" protests in these "hot spots"—led by what the federal government labelled "splinter groups" of "extremists." As INAC described in a presentation to the RCMP:

> Incidents led by splinter groups are arguably harder to manage as they exist outside negotiation processes to resolve recognized grievances with duly elected leaders. We seek to avoid giving standing to such splinter groups so as not to debase the legally recognized government. Incidents are also complicated by external groups such as Warrior Societies or non-Aboriginal counter-protest groups.

What is telling about the above INAC statement is that the identified protests were "outside of negotiation processes" with elected councils. Canada was clearly spooked by the spectre of First Nations demanding Crown recognition of Indigenous sovereignty and self-determination, as well as Aboriginal and treaty rights, beyond the narrow confines of Crown land claims and self-government policies. These so-called "splinter" groups also threatened the status quo by demanding their own First Nation leaders, staff, and advisors to pull out of the compromising negotiations.

Also telling here is the cosy co-operative relationship between INAC and the RCMP. The INAC briefing to the RCMP was almost indistinguishable from a presentation one would expect to see from security forces rather than from a government ministry. Contrary to their claims, Indian Affairs was not an institution of reconciliation and negotiation, but rather appeared to be a management office to control the costs of Native unrest. INAC was willing to work closely with law enforcement to accomplish this task.

The government treated Indigenous people who were defending their lands on a spectrum that ranged from criminals to terrorists. On either side, under Harper, an intensification of intelligence-gathering and surveillance procedures governed the new regime.

Harper appeared to be more concerned about resource companies not being blocked by First Nations than he was about Murdered and Missing Indigenous Women and Girls. This was evident from how little concern the federal government showed during the trial of Robert Pickton, who was convicted in December 2006 for murdering women and horrifically disposing of them on his pig farm near Vancouver's Downtown Eastside. This terrible tragedy triggered calls to act from Indigenous peoples to address the issue of Murdered and Missing Indigenous Women and Girls. But throughout its term, the Harper government refused to launch a public inquiry into the issue. The Harper government also ignored the Grassy Narrows Anishinaabe, who for almost fifty years called on the government to clean up mercury poisoning from their waters and territory and demanded the recognition of their land rights in the face of massive clear-cut logging of forests on their territory.

The Termination Plan Continues under Trudeau's Liberals

Harper's efforts to ignore historic treaty and inherent rights sparked the Idle No More movement in 2012. The movement created widespread awareness about Indigenous and environmental issues across Canada and influenced Justin Trudeau's platform during the 2015 election.

On the campaign trail in 2015, Trudeau's Liberals made major promises, including creating a new "nation-to-nation" process, developing a National Reconciliation Framework, enacting all 94 of the TRC's calls to action and adopting UNDRIP, establishing a national inquiry on Murdered and Missing Indigenous Women and Girls (MMIWG), and lifting the 2 percent cap on funding for First Nations funding instituted in 1995 by then Liberal Finance Minister Paul Martin.

Trudeau's "nation-to-nation" rhetoric may have convinced many Indigenous people to vote for the Liberals, but once in power, his government's policy closely resembled the termination plans of past Conservative and Liberal governments.

During Trudeau's first mandate, from 2015 through 2019, his government deployed its characteristic (and sophisticated) cocktail of slick public relations strategies and media savvy to obscure their ultimate plan: termination. Publicly, Trudeau's government announced a new, two-track national policy approach to Indigenous policy, focused on addressing socioeconomic issues in Indigenous communities and suggesting foundational changes to law and policy.

Trudeau used this two-track approach to inaugurate a massive upheaval of Indigenous law and policy, which included dissolving the Department of Indian Affairs and Northern Development and creating two new federal departments for processing Indian Act bands and band councils into a "new relationship" using what his government called "modern treaties." In sum, these modern treaties use the Comprehensive Land Claims Settlement Agreements and Self-Government Agreements as a template to terminate the preexisting sovereignty of bands and band councils. The result? These modern treaties allow the federal government to convert Indian Act bands and band councils into fourth-level ethnic "Indigenous governments," stripping them of sovereignty completely.

This plan became clear in the summer of 2016 when, at a public event in Toronto organized by *The Economist* magazine, the interviewer asked Trudeau how his government was going to liberalize and deregulate interprovincial trade within Canada. Trudeau responded: "The way to get that done is not to sit there and impose, the way to have that done is to actually have a good working relationship with the Premiers, with municipal governments, with Indigenous leadership, because Indigenous governments are the fourth level of government in this country."

As with the supposedly novel policy proposals of federal governments past, Trudeau's policy plan represents yet another attempt to end our relationship with our lands, territories, and resources.

Canada now has two new federal departments: the Department of Crown-Indigenous Relations and Northern Affairs Canada, which is tasked with negotiating and implementing these modern treaties and self-government agreements, and the Department of Indigenous Services Canada, a provisional department that will dissolve once all Indian Act bands sign modern treaties or self-government agreements and are converted into these new, fourth-level Indigenous governments.

If First Nations want to opt out of the Indian Act, they have three options. The first option is to sign a legally binding modern treaty, which, as described above, is a fast track to the termination of sovereignty. The second is to sign a Self-Government Agreement, which will subject them to the federal and provincial powers under the Canadian Constitution. However, under this option, the First Nation would be considered a fourth order of government—below not only the federal and provincial governments, but also with less power than municipal governments. Or, the final option: assimilation into Canada's property and tax systems through the First Nations Land Management Act and the First Nations Fiscal Management Act.

In 2017, the Liberals and the AFN agreed to a series of "joint priorities" for Indigenous policy, formalized in the AFN-Canada Memorandum of Understanding (MOU) on Joint Priorities. The MOU creates a national, top-down process and codifies the new "nation-to-nation" relationship Trudeau's government is pursuing with First Nations. While Trudeau has branded this agreement as evidence of his government's co-operative approach to the co-development of Indigenous policy, the federal government maintains an effective veto over the MOU priorities, implementation, and funding. In their 2019 platform, the federal Liberals reference this MOU—evidence that Trudeau's second mandate will be as fraught as his first.

Indigenous communities and First Nations are caught in a legal and political bind—there is no good route out of the colonial Indian Act, yet there is no manoeuvring within the Act's colonial framework either.

This is re-colonization, not self-determination, and we need a new approach. Indigenous communities should be able to develop their own local and regional self-determination plans to provide alternatives to Canada's National Reconciliation Plan, which has turned out to be just a rebranding of the age-old federal termination plan.

I believe all Indigenous nations need to build the foundation of their nationhood on free, prior, informed consent before they sit down with the government to begin true nation-to-nation negotiations.

What is certain is that by standing together and developing an Indigenous agenda based on our rights as set out under international law, Indigenous groups can advance a future for our peoples much more effectively than by passively accepting the federal government's watered down and self-serving version of our rights that the current AFN leadership seems prepared to accept.

We are told by governments, and too often by our own leadership, that there is no alternative to the cookie-cutter surrender of lands and resources provided at the existing government negotiation tables. The fact is that we do have another course of action, one that is supported by the international laws that recognize the right of all peoples to self-determination.

My vision is to see First Nations protect their traditional lands and waters by developing and implementing their own self-determination plans for community development and nationhood based on restoration of stolen lands, territories and resources, or restitution where lands and resources aren't returned.

The fact is, before reconciliation there has to be truth.

Portions of this essay originally appeared in an article co-written with Shiri Pasternak titled "Canada Has Had First Nations Under Surveillance: Harper Government Has Prepared for First Nations 'Unrest,'" published in the First Nations Strategic Bulletin 9, no. 1–5, January-May 2011.

2006 | Oaxaca: From State of Siege to Police State

Emilie Teresa Smith

Outside, the streets are dark and terrifying. We slink in the shadows as truck after truck of police search the streets.

This article was written as a letter to my loved ones back home in Canada from the front lines of the struggle in Oaxaca, in southern Mexico, in the last days of November 2006. I am a Canadian-raised Anglican priest, born in Argentina and formed as a Christian in the liberation struggles in Central America. My whole adult life I have come alongside communities fighting to overthrow their historical oppressors, and for most of 2006, I found myself working with Indigenous youth from Oaxaca. That year, teachers and Indigenous leaders had come together to oppose the centuries of abuse, oppression, and exclusion that had crushed their communities.

I first visited Oaxaca in February of 2006, and then six Oaxacan youth lived with me for the month of June—in Canada for a peace conference. I returned to Oaxaca for the month of August. Finally, in early November, I rushed down again when my beloved friend Rosario (nickname Chayo)—a Mixtec Indigenous law student—phoned me in terror. Government thugs had just murdered Brad Will, a journalist from the US, who had been staying at their community home on the outskirts of Oaxaca City. By that time, the city had been completely taken over by the rebels who had created APPO, the Popular Oaxacan Peoples' Association, and were occupying the plazas and barricading the highways while government forces closed in. On Saturday, November 25, the final assault took place, and the PFP, the National Preventive Police (militarized antiriot forces), crushed the opposition, killing some, arresting dozens.

This account is from a collection of letters I wrote, later self-published as a book, *The Haunted Banana Trees of Dragón Barricada*. My year in and out of Oaxaca changed me. I began to write and publish regularly about liberation struggles, and in 2009 I returned to live for four years in the south, in Guatemala. In 2012, I became co-president of the historic liberation theology network SICSAL, following the enormous footsteps of my beloved grandfather, jTatic Samuel Ruiz, Bishop of Chiapas, who in November 2006 had intervened for peace in the Oaxaca uprising. I have returned to Oaxaca several times, and I maintain regular contact with the youth I befriended there in 2006. The teachers and Indigenous leaders continue to fight for justice in their communities.

November 29, 2006

One more horrible night is over, and the sun is up in the east (as usual). The man who sweeps the streets in front of the house just went by. I "slept" fitfully, in my clothes and boots. Dragón Barricada, the yellow puppy I rescued from the barricades at the university, is curled up in a ball on my blanket. I'm on guard duty, and I've just walked the whole compound, and out back. All is normal. Will the threats we get on the eerie phone calls late at night be carried out, or is it just to scare us? I don't know. Houses around the city are being broken into or burnt to the ground by government-sponsored thugs. I don't know why we've escaped so far.

The days after the march—November 25, when the police carried out their final attack—Sunday, Monday, and yesterday have been marked by fear.

The violence of Saturday was the terror we had all been dreading. It was a confusing scene, but basically it breaks down like this: there were hundreds of thousands of peaceful protesters, mostly teachers, people who came down from the Indigenous communities, women, and others. They were marching—peacefully—to the Zocalo, the central plaza.

There were some—a very, very small minority of what I would describe as hot-headed youth—who, in their frustrated youthful way, really wanted to do battle with the authorities. The APPO error was not containing this element, though I witnessed many of the older, wiser protesters speaking calmly and firmly to this group. Several provocateurs in the crowd were there precisely to push people on to violence, for which the repercussions were to be horrendous.

There is lack of clarity as to who began the violence: protesters with rocks or the PFP from the rooftops, which is most often reported.

However the violence began, the police reaction was way out of proportion, resulting in the wounding of several hundred people, and the detention and torture of many more. These initial acts of violence, which involved a small minority of protesters, provided the authorities with exactly the excuse they needed to close down absolutely every site of legitimate protest. And that is what they are doing.

That is why I describe Oaxaca as having moved from a state of siege to a police state. I don't know what to compare it to—Nazi Germany, Soviet Russia, Guatemala in the 1970s at the beginning of the repression, before the genocide. Now the police control the Zocalo, the Plaza Santo Domingo, the parks, in reality, the whole city—except the university. They move by day and by night in trucks, sometimes in uniform, often not.

Arbitrary detentions are constant, and torture is almost universal along with detentions. Mostly women, and some men, have been raped. Plainclothes government thugs have free range to do as they will. The priest of Seven Principes, one of the churches that offered first aid to protesters on Saturday night, one of the churches I criticized for not doing enough, was shot at on Monday.

Medical students are another particular target. Three people were shot and killed outside the medical building on Saturday night. On Monday, right during a press conference to denounce the shooting, government thugs showed up and right then and there dragged off one youth. The whole affair was captured on camera and published in the paper. He wasn't even arrested, he just simply disappeared.

Human rights groups are being attacked, as are the women's organizations, and as usual, especially Indigenous rights groups. It is an absolutely terrifying time in the history of this struggle. The hunt is on for all leaders of APPO elected at the recent Congress.

The university is the only safe spot, but under constant threat of attack. (Later, on Wednesday, November 30, the barricades protecting the university were taken down). I was there late on Monday afternoon, and it is a sad, sad place, a place under siege. Night descends, and we hear the eerie sound of the conch shell, an ancient Indigenous way of communicating. The last holdouts in the barricades are calling out to one another.

Satanas, a veterinary student and leader of the resistance, asks me to take two street kids home with me, and I agree. They'd been living well in the university barricade for months, but all this is coming to an end. I invite them, come on *mucha*, come with me, but they refuse to leave, what and miss the last battle? I hug goodbye to Lola and Miguel—the main leaders I have been accompanying for a month, they're staying here, the last safe place. My heart sinks, and I eat back my tears as we move—Chayo and I—out past the barricade, leaving them, and all the rest, and the children, and the last puppy.

Outside, the streets are dark and terrifying. We slink in the shadows as truck after truck of police search the streets. As we get to the house, a pickup truck pulls up right behind us, and out leap seven men. They are so obviously armed and dangerous. We wait before moving on, and they go up the street. Others are with them. I count at least ten or twelve.

The next day, we get to an emergency meeting with as many surviving leaders as can safely gather. It seems, however, that a military block has prevented most of the delegates from the Sierra Juarez. ¡Tatic is here! (Bishop Samuel Ruiz, my grandfather). It is such a relief to see him and to feel his calm, faithful presence. He holds me in an embrace and blesses my head. Later on the government radio, there is a call to attack the Indigenous leaders who had gathered that day, and a prize for anyone who can kill the Bishop. My heart aches in the face of such hatred. We hear again and again the story of these months of struggle as part of a much bigger struggle that the Indigenous communities have been carrying on for centuries. Again, the focus is on Indigenous community autonomy, how that can be carried forward into these different times, with everything shut down.

We come home before dark this time, carrying our agony into another night of anxious waiting. We have a plan now, escape routes marked and ready, and basically, we're just resigned. Only Chayo, Pedro, and I are left in the safe house. We tour out and around the back. We turn on all the lights. Chayo braids my hair. The wind picks up, rustling through the haunted banana trees, and we all sit a bit closer together.

Originally published on December 1, 2006.

2007 | After the Pickton Trial, What Lives On?

Amber Dean

> "We inherit not "what really happened" to the dead but what lives on from that happening, what is conjured from it, how past generations and events occupy the force fields of the present, how they claim us, and how they haunt, plague, and inspirit our imaginations and visions for the future."
>
> —Wendy Brown, *Politics Out of History*

After several years spent researching the events surrounding the disappearances and deaths of so many women from Vancouver's Downtown Eastside, there is only one thing I know for sure: that knowing "what really happened" to those women does little to help us struggle with the stunning complexity of "what lives on from that happening."

This is the thought that kept running through my head last January, as I sat in shocked silence in the overflow courtroom in New Westminster, BC on the first day of Robert William Pickton's trial for the murders of Sereena Abotsway, Mona Wilson, Andrea Joesbury, Marnie Frey, Brenda Wolfe, and Georgina Papin.

I thought I was prepared that day for what I was about to hear, as I was no stranger to the circumstances surrounding the trial. But as I listened to Crown counsel describe, in the cold, matter-of-fact language of legalese, "what really happened" to those six women, I knew that I was not prepared, not at all. And I wondered how knowing this information could make any difference to the injustices the women experienced, injustices which continue to shape the present.

Now that the trial is over and this lone individual has been convicted and sent to prison for the rest of his life, there is a sense that we can "move on," that with the verdict comes "closure." I am in awe of the family members who stuck through this trial, and I am grateful that the verdict has given some of them a sense of relief. I also know that some media commentators made an effort to point out that little has changed for women in the Downtown Eastside in the years since Pickton's arrest. A spattering of stories along these lines appeared in the day or two after the verdict and sentencing. They've all but disappeared now, though, which is unfortunate, since what lives on from the deaths of so many women has everything to do with the ongoing injustices evident in this neighbourhood.

Family members of the disappeared women, Downtown Eastside activists, and some politicians and journalists have called for increased funding and support for women in the Downtown Eastside, increased protections for women doing sex work, and an investigation into how the police (mis)handled reports of women going missing from the neighbourhood. All of these are extremely important. But what I think most of us have yet to consider are the social dimensions of the suffering and loss that has taken place. In other words, how are we all implicated in the disappearances and deaths of so many women, even if we live hundreds of kilometres away and had no prior relationship with them? How are these events both written and sustained by the arrangements of our social world?

Let me give you an example. There has been a noticeable shift in mainstream media representations of the women who were disappeared. Early descriptions emphasized how the women were "prostitutes" and "drug addicts," while recent descriptions tend to focus more on the women's roles as mothers, sisters, and daughters. This shift has come about mainly through the determination of the women's family members, who refused to let the world know their loved ones only through such narrow descriptions of how they lived their lives. But why did we need to know that the women were also mothers, sisters, and daughters in order to care about their fate? Does this imply that generally speaking, many of us don't consider people labelled "prostitutes" and "drug addicts" to be worthy of our concern? What might this shift then tell us about the assumptions that underpin our social world and our everyday interactions with others?

The mainstream media has also paid little attention to the fact that the women who were disappeared from the Downtown Eastside were disproportionately Indigenous. This fact makes me wonder how European colonization and settlement of the land now known as Canada is related to this present-day violence.

Of course, it's often said that the past is, well, *past*, that what happened in the past is over, finished, done, relevant to the present only in the form of a history lesson. According to that logic, colonization is a completed project. It is something we might lament or decry, but it's seldom thought to be ongoing in the present. And yet Vancouver's Downtown Eastside is often talked about today using the language and metaphors of the Frontier; it is repeatedly described as a kind of "Wild West" zone.

These descriptions invite us to imagine the Downtown Eastside as a bordered space that is ripe for conquest and resettlement. This happens not only through media representations, but also through plans to "clean up" and "bring order" to the neighbourhood, and through efforts to gentrify it (which are all happening right now at an alarming pace in advance of the 2010 Olympics). So, I wonder: what is the relationship between these descriptions that invite a new "conquest" of the land and the terrible violence inflicted disproportionately on Indigenous women from this neighbourhood?

A lot of emphasis has been put on getting us to think about "what really happened" to the women who were murdered. Learning the Crown's version of what really happened to the women at the opening of the trial, and learning it again and again in countless media representations of those facts, has done nothing to help me confront the staggering realities of these events. In fact, those sensational details might distract us from the more difficult but perhaps more important task of thinking about what lives on from that happening.

Despite the conclusion of Pickton's first trial, I'm far from certain that we now know (or can ever know) all of "what really happened" to allow so many women to disappear for such a long stretch of time.

This doesn't mean that we shouldn't try to find out. But perhaps now that the trial is over we might shift our attention to what lives on, in the interests of a present (and future) that might be otherwise.

Originally published on December 20, 2007.

2008 | From Queen's Park to Grassy Narrows: Organizing to Win

Carmelle Wolfson

> "I heard it on the television
> All the talking politicians
> Words are easy, words are cheap
> Much cheaper than our priceless land
> But promises can disappear
> Just like writing in the sand"
>
> —Australian musician Yothu Yindi

For years, every level of Canadian government has made assurances to the First Nations that were never carried out. But in just a couple of weeks, we've seen amazing gains for First Nations communities in Ontario. Indigenous leaders arrested for protesting mining on their lands have been freed from jail. The third-largest logging company in North America has been driven away by resistance from the First Nations community that stakes claim on that land. Finally, diverse communities, organizations, and individuals who have been hesitant to work together in the past are working hand-in-hand for Indigenous land rights.

Sleepover for Sovereignty at Queen's Park

The Gathering of Mother Earth Protectors and Sovereignty Sleepover took place from May 26 to 29, 2008, at Queen's Park, but given the events of the past few weeks, it feels like it's still ongoing. We were calling on the provincial government to respect the right to say no to environmental destruction on Indigenous lands. We were demanding freedom for political prisoners Robert Lovelace, former chief of Ardoch Algonquin First Nation, and six community members from Kitchenuhmaykoosib Inninuwug (KI) First Nation. Lovelace and the KI-6 each spent several months in jail after blocking the activities of mining companies on their lands.

The gathering culminated with Grassy Narrows, Ardoch Algonquin, and KI First Nations and their supporters grasping hands to make a wish before offering tobacco into the sacred fire. Then we headed off for the final march. Normally, I would find this kind of stuff pretty cheesy, but somehow it just seemed like the right thing to do. The gesture was a spiritual custom from a First Nations tradition but also symbolized disparate groups coming together to form a broad coalition.

Allies came from across Ontario to attend the gathering. KI community members travelled from one of the most remote communities in northern Ontario's boreal forest, while more than twenty Grassy Narrows folks walked from Kenora nearly two thousand kilometres along the highway. The trek took almost four weeks.

There was a general sense of optimism in the air as activists reunited with one another at the May 26 rally. It had been two years since I, along with a group of Rainforest Action Network (RAN) interns, camped out at the Slant Lake Blockade in Grassy Narrows. The First Nations community has been holding down the longest logging blockade in history to protect their traditional lands—used by local community members for hunting and harvesting berries and medicinal herbs—from clear-cut logging practices. Two years since the Earth Justice Gathering in Grassy saw over one hundred activists from across the continent hold a twelve-hour blockade on the Trans-Canada Highway. It was good to see everyone together again in one place. Even though it was Queen's Park, it felt like our own private party space (replete with rented party tents, a mobile stage, a sound system and three cooked meals served up every day).

While the high profile speakers (comedian Cathy Jones, novelist Thomas King, Christian Peacemaker Teams [CPT] member James Loney, and former AFN chief Ovide Mercredi) and the CLC-endorsed two thousand-strong march on May 29 were the events most people heard about, it was the time spent in between where the real coalition-building took place.

A Broad Coalition Taking Direction from First Nations Communities

During the daily teach-ins, participants had the chance to learn about wide-ranging issues from the locally specific (the politics surrounding the arrest of Tyendinaga Mohawk Shawn Brant) to the far-reaching (the links between the Olympics, the G8 and the Security and Prosperity Partnership of North America). More importantly, we all had a chance to make lasting connections and discuss future action plans. Meetings and consultations are already underway in southern Ontario for a 2010 resistance.

The weeks leading up to the Sovereignty Sleepover were filled with endless conference calls (Monday, rally and sleepover coordination, Tuesday, sovereignty sleepover logistics, Friday, community and organization representatives). At Queen's Park, we finally had the chance to meet face-to-face. The coinciding Canadian Labour Congress (CLC) convention offered an opportunity for union backing. While union members were less present at the campout, many endorsed the Gathering of Mother Earth Protectors, including OPSEU, CUPE, OSSTF, the Law Union of Ontario, and of course the CLC itself. Prior to the event, CPT and others allied with religious organizations like the Anglican Council of Indigenous Peoples, the National Indigenous Anglican Bishop, United Churches Bloor and Spadina, and the Toronto Buddhist Peace Fellowship for endorsements and resources.

Key organizers considered the diversity of groups involved as well as how high the stakes were for the three First Nations communities. In response, they worked out a framework to deal with important tactical questions. Non-Indigenous supporters would take direction from KI, Ardoch, and Grassy Narrows community leaders. Other groups provided logistical support in Toronto, including RAN, CPT, ForestEthics, the Canadian Federation of Students, the Ontario Coalition Against Poverty, the Tyendinaga Support Committee, No One Is Illegal, and the Coalition Against Israeli Apartheid.

A conscious effort was made to take lessons learned from the 2006 Earth Justice Gathering to inform the way we organized this one. Everyone attempted to be inclusive and transparent in organizing this event. Security liaisons engaged in open dialogue with Queen's Park, negotiating the use of the front lawn to light a sacred fire and erect teepees, party tents, and mosquito mesh tents for people to "rest their eyes" (the words of QP officials who didn't want to admit they were permitting us to sleep onsite).

Michael Bryant, provincial Minister of Aboriginal affairs, came out front of Queen's Park for a few brief moments to give interviews with the media but didn't talk to any gathering participants. He reiterated that ye olde Mining Act should be revised. The Act doesn't take into consideration outstanding Indigenous land claims and allows companies to set up shop on private property belonging to settlers since they own only the surface rights.

Movement Building Leads to Victories

But politicians' tokenistic gestures don't encompass the true power of the movement itself. The events of the last few weeks speak for themselves. The first and second victories came simultaneously on Wednesday, May 28. While the harsh sentencing of the seven Indigenous leaders was clearly politically motivated, justice was finally served when Robert Lovelace *and* the KI-6 (Donny Morris, Cecilia Begg, Sam McKay, Jack McKay, Darryl Sainnawap, and Bruce Sakakeep) were all freed from prison.

The courthouse was so packed that supporters spilled out onto the street. Bob Lovelace, the KI-6, and lawyer Chris Reid joined the crowd at Queen's Park to celebrate immediately following their release.

Although uranium mining continues at the Robertsville site near Ardoch and Sharbot Lake, a precedent was set in the Ontario Court of Appeals when Lovelace was released. In response, Frontenac Ventures dropped the remaining injunction charges on June 2 against him and other activists charged for protesting against the mine. Victory number three!

The final and most extraordinary victory came on June 3, when one of the largest paper and pulp corporations in the world, AbitibiBowater, announced they would halt logging in Grassy Narrows and pursue alternative wood sources. The Slant Lake blockade at Grassy Narrows is the longest standing in Canada. Five and a half years of blockades in the community and solidarity actions targeting companies that AbitibiBowater supplies have crippled the logging industry in the Whiskey Jack Forest. In February, Boise announced they would no longer purchase wood fibre coming from Grassy Narrows. AbitibiBowater says they cannot wait four more years while the province negotiates with the Grassy Narrows council.

"Now they can't say direct action doesn't work," a friend told me following the announcement. If something has been learned from the Grassy Narrows victory, KI and Ardoch will regain control over their lands.

RAN, CPT, Amnesty International, ForestEthics and others have all worked in solidarity with the Grassy Narrows community to fight destructive logging on their traditional lands. The unrelenting Grassy blockade in conjunction with outside supporters pressuring companies in urban centres meant they literally couldn't afford to ignore us. Opposition to corporate greed and injustice need not remain a localized issue. Our personal connections could not be broken by distance alone.

A Peruvian from a community with the largest gold mines in South America said it very eloquently at the May 26 rally: "The Andean people are united with Canada's First Nations people to defend their water and their land." He went on to say, "This economic system that's based on greed wants to take away from us not only our land but also our spirit and our unity. And we're here to make sure that doesn't happen."

Through our solidarity networks, we were able to break the isolation that can hinder resistance. Our arms stretched across rivers and highways. There were times when we as activists had tactical disagreements, but we recognized that this issue was too important to walk away from. When we build solidarity instead of division within our movements, we can accomplish so much more.

When we held hands at Queen's Park, we were told to make a wish. I wished for logging to stop in Grassy Narrows. It looks like I wasn't the only one.

Originally published on June 18, 2008.

2009 | Imagine: Prosperity without Growth

Murray Dobbin

It is ironic that *homo sapiens*, we big-brained and clever species, can trace almost every tragedy and failing to one generic cause: a failure of imagination.

We seem to be an idiot savant species—stunningly clever at so many things, capable of greatness, creativity, and sacrifice for others, melding genius and love when we are at our best, and greed and hate at our worst.

But whether it is the individual who fails to imagine the consequences of punching someone in a bar or a whole society (like California) which fails to imagine the consequences of starving itself of the revenue needed to function, observers from another world could easily conclude that we are terminally stupid. Or, as John Ralston Saul put, unconscious as a civilization.

Those individuals and organizations who have fought off the madness and ruin of neoliberal policies for over twenty years are now presented with the best possible time to present a vision of what is possible.

Washington Consensus Exposed As a Pack of Lies

Globalization is effectively dead: what characterized the world for the past thirty years, the suicidal policies of what was called the Washington Consensus, will never return, at least not in their old form. The climate crisis, the damage done to the real economies of the Global North, the arrival of peak oil, the inevitable return of protectionism, and state intervention mean that we have left that era behind.

Not only has financial capitalism and its corruption and ersatz wealth been exposed. The Chicago boys, the intellectual storm troopers in the free market think tanks and editorial writers of Asper media are facing an ideological crisis. The whole edifice stands exposed as a pack of lies and deceptions created for the sole purpose of enriching the already wealthy.

"There is no alternative." Really? There had bloody well better be or we are all doomed. "Government is the problem, not the solution"? The banks and the CEOs of the transnationals who revelled in this slogan would now disagree. And what about the cause of the evil deficits—governments "spending like drunken sailors"? Now Bay Street believes that government isn't nearly drunk enough. And the demand that we "run government like a business"? Just which bankrupt, crooked, reckless business would that be?

The magnitude of the moral crisis of the political right is staggering. The greed, dishonesty, hubris, and psychopathic disregard for the public good renders the whole business elite utterly unfit to pronounce on anything—not even on the economy, but certainly not democracy or how we run our collective affairs.

Denial and Complacency in the Face of Crisis

All of this should add up to the biggest opportunity the left has had in over a generation to take the lead, to frame the issues in terms of Canadians' stated values and aspirations, to bury the Washington Consensus ideology in the rubble of its own destructive legacy. This is our opportunity. These two crises have arrived just in time to wake us up, just in time for us to choose to save the planet and ourselves from a truly grim future. Not just rising oceans and the loss of coastal communities, but a nightmarish dystopia characterized by global social unrest, the rise of fascism, mass starvation, and wars over energy and water.

But to date, there is silence.

Most middle-class people—and this includes the majority of social and political activists—are still acting as if this is just another recession. We'll just eat out less and take a two-week vacation instead of four until it blows over. The concession to the moral crisis of climate change is to buy a Prius and think we have made a difference. This is denial on a gargantuan scale. If every gas guzzler were replaced tomorrow by a Prius, we would still have ten times too many private cars on the road.

In the US, there is a growing movement to cut taxes—in a country starved for social programs, with an education system barely competing with Botswana's, and an almost unimaginable debt counted in the tens of trillions of dollars. The US is headed for the most catastrophic collapse of empire in human history. Canada is not quite as delusional, but we are still a nation in denial, determined to maintain an insane consumer culture, and damn the consequences for ourselves and future generations.

Leadership Lacking

The current situation is not a normal crisis—it is a world-changing shift that could go in any of several directions. It cannot remain static, and without progressive leadership, it is certain to go badly. But where is that leadership? It is not coming from traditional sources. Organized labour is, understandably, preoccupied with saving threatened industries. (No talk there of forcing the Big Three to focus their massive infrastructure and technical know-how on mass transit. And no government commitment to expand it.)

Social movement organizations are fighting the usual single-issue battles as if the context had not changed at all. The environmental movement still resists the fact that dealing with climate change without addressing social and economic democracy is impossible.

And the political parties who should be providing a vision for a better future are mired in tactical politics. Jack Layton dismisses Michael Ignatieff's musing about the need for future tax increases as "old school" and suggests that the solution is to "grow the economy."

The planet will not survive "growing the economy." In its current trajectory, our world is terminal with the cancer of rampant consumerism metastasizing to every living system we need to survive. Sixty percent of the world's ecosystems are currently degraded.

The stupendous "growth" of the last twenty years has seen the rich get filthy rich and the poor get poorer, with 20 percent of the global population subsisting on 2 percent of the world's resources. Canadian families have rung up unprecedented debt trying to maintain a middle-class consumer lifestyle that doesn't even make them happy.

Buying a hybrid car isn't going to cut it. Indeed nothing short of a cultural revolution in the developed world has any chance of saving the planet and humanity. How will we know that the revolution is underway? When there is a movement not to cut taxes but to ban advertising. When there is a massive call for taxing wealth so that no individual can take more than, say, $100,000 a year out of our collective wealth. When mandatory Sunday closing returns and families spend time together outside the shopping mall. When there is no more talk of ending poverty and homelessness, because it will have disappeared. When we willingly—no, eagerly—pay half our income in taxes so that we can have the things we actually say we want as a community.

We need, on the left, to once again become the source of Big Ideas. Our defensive politics of the last twenty-five years has dulled our imaginations to the point of stagnation. We are leading from behind. So-called ordinary Canadians are desperate for a vision of the future they can grasp on to and believe is possible. We have given them more of the same: the politics of despair, telling struggling working people that things are actually worse than they already think they are.

We are obsessed with "stimulating" the economy. Instead, we need to have a national conversation about starving the beast. Capitalism must grow to survive, and no matter how we tweak this perverse system, growth will ensure its continued social and environmental destruction. Growing the economy in the face of this crisis is madness: doing the same thing over and over again and expecting different results. Fortunately, there are people thinking about this under the umbrella notion of "prosperity without growth."

Amazingly, the British government has put together a whole website full of ideas and debates about what this might look like. A project of the Sustainable Development Commission, it suggests that creating conditions for people to flourish "includes tackling systemic inequality and removing incentives for unproductive status competition; sharing available work and improving work-life balance and reversing the culture of consumerism; building a sustainable macro-economy which is no longer structurally reliant on increasing consumption."

In Canada, there is the just-started, three-year Climate Justice Project of the BC office of the CCPA. It promises to engage in groundbreaking research on climate change but through the lens of social justice.

There are others, as well. In Paris last year, the Economic De-Growth for Ecological Sustainability and Social Equity Conference came up with a declaration about the world of the future. Among its many articles, two stand out as characterizing the kind of thinking that must start spreading. De-growth in the global North, says the declaration, "is characterized by substantially reduced dependence on economic activity, and an increase in free time, unremunerated activity, conviviality, sense of community and individual and collective health; [and the] encouragement of self-reflection, balance, creativity, flexibility, diversity, good citizenship, generosity and non-materialism."

Everyone put their Blackberrys down. Go to these sites. Send them to friends.

To be fair, progressive organizations are exhausted and demoralized. Fighting trench warfare and rearguard actions against a powerful and ruthless adversary for twenty-five years will do that to individuals and organizations. But we will not find new energy and inspiration in the trenches—and we won't inspire others from there either.

Canadians' values are amazingly progressive, but a generation of neoliberal assaults has lowered their expectations of what is possible. Nevertheless, they are out there waiting for someone, anyone, to present them with reasons to be hopeful. What they want and what we need is what America's radical rabbi, Michael Lerner, calls the politics of meaning. More on that next time.

Originally published on June 19, 2009.

2010 | Stop Canada's Cultural Genocide at Barriere Lake

Corvin Russell

Canada and Quebec are waging a war of attrition on a small band of five hundred Algonquins a few hours north of Ottawa. Today, this war has reached a critical juncture: its outcome will be a judgment on whether Canada is able to share the land with First Nations while respecting their right to maintain their cultures and determine their own destinies, or whether Canada can only offer resilient Aboriginal cultures a menu of assimilation, dependency, and cultural death.

The community of the Algonquins of Barriere Lake stands out as one of the few road-accessible First Nations in Canada that has largely retained its language, traditional economy and knowledge, and customary form of government. Children still speak Algonquin. People still hunt, fish, and gather traditional foods and medicines. Traditional artifacts, even birch bark canoes, continue to be made. The community is one of only 26 First Nations in Canada (out of more than 630) that fully govern themselves by their customs. The Algonquins of Barriere Lake have survived as an Aboriginal culture because of a determination to hold on to their identity and preserve their relationship to their traditional lands, which provide them life and sustenance.

This stubbornness has made them very inconvenient for Canada and Quebec, who see the Algonquins of Barriere Lake as obstructing unfettered access to profit-generating resources on Algonquin land. For decades, Canada and Quebec have engaged in a drawn-out political, economic, bureaucratic, and legal strategy to force them into submission. In 1991, after years of blockades and political struggle, the Algonquins of Barriere Lake reached an agreement with the governments of Canada and Quebec that would allow for revenue sharing, sustainable resource co-management, and economic independence for Barriere Lake. But Canada has not honoured this agreement. Because Barriere Lake did not surrender Aboriginal title to its lands in this agreement, Canada sees the agreement as a threat to its Indian policy, which has always been about one thing: getting control of all Indian lands and extinguishing Aboriginal title everywhere. Canada and Quebec do not want to share land or revenues with First Nations.

Canada stopped paying the monies it owes Barriere Lake under this "Trilateral Agreement" in 2001 and has kept the community in a state of impoverishment. Quebec stopped paying implementation monies in 2007 and has never paid the royalties it owes under the agreement. Recently, the Canadian government used the band's deteriorating fiscal position, caused in part by nonpayment of monies from Canada and Quebec, as a pretext to impose "third-party management," under which the band is administered by a private firm of white accountants in Quebec City who know nothing of Algonquin culture, who do not spend time in the community, and who are paid handsomely out of the band's meagre budget. (This firm was not selected through a transparent process, and there is no public accountability for its actions.)

Canada has worked to undermine the community at every turn, criminalizing community members for defending their rights, subjecting them to police brutality, and keeping the community mired in court processes.

In its most recent gambit, the Department of Indian Affairs used an archaic section of the Indian Act, last forcibly used in 1924 against the people of Six Nations when they were campaigning internationally to get their sovereignty and rights recognized. Under Section 74 of the Indian Act, Indian Affairs has imposed on the Algonquins of Barriere Lake a system of government more convenient to Canada—one that gives people living off-territory the power to choose the community leadership and run for office, even though they have the least stakes in the maintenance of the community's land base and culture. By contrast, under Barriere Lake's customary governance code, participation in leadership selections is open only to those band members who live in the traditional territory and have knowledge of and connection to the land.

Canada claims that it must impose the Indian Act government on the Algonquins of Barriere Lake because their traditional system doesn't work and because the community is divided. But what community, Indigenous or not, is not divided? This does not give Indian Affairs the right to meddle in First Nations' government. As community spokesperson Marylynn Poucachiche says, "in fact it's the government's interference in our internal affairs that has destabilized our governance." And, contrary to the ministry's claims, all major factions of the community are united in opposition to the imposition of Ottawa's system. Even Indian Affairs admits that only "between six and ten" community members out of several hundred participated in the Indian Affairs band council selection process. Even though most community members boycotted the process, Indian Affairs claims this council is "more democratic" than the traditional government. Casey Ratt, who was acclaimed as chief—no vote was ever held—refused the position. The Ottawa-imposed council is still operating without a chief and holding its meetings off-territory, signing logging permits and making other decisions that affect the community, without a mandate.

Canada and the Algonquins of Barriere Lake agree on one thing: the customary government of Barriere Lake is one of the sources of the community's strength in resisting assimilation. As Poucachiche says, "the real reason they are imposing band elections is to sever our connection to the land, which is maintained by our traditional political system. They don't want to deal with a strong leadership and a community that demands governments honour its signed agreements regarding the exploitation of our lands and resources." That's why the white government has decided the customary Algonquin government must go.

Today, the people of Barriere Lake travelled en masse to Ottawa to protest the Canadian government's attack on their community and lands. Algonquin youth are leading the fight to uphold their traditions. The community has promised it will not allow the Indian Act system to be imposed by the white government. The Algonquins of Barriere Lake have never consented, by treaty or any other agreement, to be subject to the Indian Act. Barriere Lake's inherent right to customary self-government is protected by section 35 of the Canadian Constitution and enshrined in the United Nations Declaration on the Rights of Indigenous Peoples. A May 2010 report by the Standing Senate Committee on Aboriginal Peoples affirmed that First Nations have the right to maintain control over their internal affairs and to be free to pursue their vision of customary government. The Assembly of First Nations has passed a unanimous resolution condemning the government and demanding that the Minister of Indian Affairs rescind the band elections imposed through section 74 of the Indian Act.

The Harper government has made a great show of verbal apologies to Aboriginal peoples for the atrocities Canada committed in the past. Many noble sentiments have been expressed about refounding the relationship between Canada and Aboriginal Peoples on the basis of respect. Last month, the Harper government gave a qualified endorsement of the United Nations Declaration on the Rights of Indigenous Peoples (UNDRIP). Yet at Barriere Lake, Canada and Quebec are doing exactly what they have been doing for more than 150 years: ruthlessly pursuing a policy of assimilation and cultural genocide in order to secure access to profitable resources without sharing the benefits with the Indigenous people they belong to. Meanwhile, the Algonquins are upholding the lands for all of us, Native and non-Native.

Barriere Lake is a signpost for the future of Canada-Indigenous relations. It is time for the people of Quebec and Canada to give meaning to all the noble words and promises and fulfil the guarantees our Constitution has made to Aboriginal peoples. It is time for us to tell our governments: stop the cultural genocide of Aboriginal peoples. Honour your word. And respect the rights of Indigenous peoples, once and for all.

Originally published on December 13, 2010.

2011–2014 | Section 3: Combatting Neoliberalism

There Is an Alternative

Michael Stewart

Around the second decade of the twenty-first century, a new word emerged to describe the contemporary experience of neoliberalism: precarity. Stephen Harper had already been prime minister for five years and had continued the thirty-year-old austerity project of his Liberal and Conservative predecessors, from Brian Mulroney to Paul Martin. What was left of Canada's welfare state had been ground down to the barest rock, and it was getting harder and harder to draw blood from stone.

A job-seeking friend—who happens to have a PhD but can't find work in his field—was applying for a "content editor" position with a marketing firm. One of the requisite qualifications was the ability to "function in an ambiguous environment with ever-changing expectations." Never had a job requirement, he remarked, come so close to identifying one of the causes of his intermittent, existential dread.

The experience of precarity is borne of two things: one, deep-seated anxiety that one or more of your basic needs—food, shelter, companionship—is either at risk or can't be met at all; and two, not knowing when or if this sense of uncertainty will ever end. It should come as no surprise then that the capacity to endure a precarious world—or to "function in an ambiguous environment with ever-changing expectations," to coin a phrase—should become a qualification for the type of job that helped create it in the first place.

The future has always been, to some degree, uncertain, particularly for low-income or marginalized people. All wage labour, after all, is precarious. A young worker in the 1980s may have feared getting laid off; people of colour and Indigenous people faced discrimination and abuse; women faced double standards at home, in public, and in the workplace. There has always been a dividing line between those protected by the state or by wealth, those who are protected by white supremacy, settler colonialism, patriarchy, and heteronormativity, and those who are not.

What makes precarity different is that those who feel its effects *don't know* if they are protected or not. This was the goal of the Harper years, 2006–15: division, disorder, and a state of constant tumult. Young people earned jobs that were never meant to be permanent in the first place; they rented homes in buildings that could be replaced by high-street condos at any time; they lived in towns with transient populations where neighbourly interaction seemed like an unaffordable frivolity; and they were slowly realizing that they inhabited a planet where climate scientists foretold a future bleaker than any Cormac McCarthy novel.

Organized labour has, for the better part of a century, done its part to protect us from the brutalities of capital. Workplace protections, social welfare, and democratic representation for those who generate wealth in this country against those who seize it—these are the fruits of collective bargaining, not just for unionized workers but for all of us. But three decades of austerity extracted a blood price. Bleary-eyed and battered, unions were no longer fighting for new rights, new protections. They were fighting tooth and nail to cling to the scraps that hadn't yet been parcelled out to private capital.

There are two arms of neoliberalism, both equally ruthless. One arm seeks to transfer wealth from the workforce to private hands: to move public institutions into for-profit arenas, eradicate the welfare state, and create an increasingly vulnerable workforce. Though substantively diminished from their heyday, unions did their best to resist. But per the other arm of neoliberalism, the rhetorical arm, unions were not ready for what would come. Canada's corporate media and other opinion makers shifted the terms of our social contract. Union leaders were reframed as out-of-touch bureaucrats, and neoliberal fictions like Trudeau's Minister of Middle Class Prosperity emerged to pretend to help protect working people while union density stagnated.

The language war was rapid and fierce. Neoliberalism forced us to retreat into ourselves for solutions no longer offered, supported, or even acknowledged by the state or collective bargaining. Instead of vulnerable, our workers become "flexible." Work became gigs, job churn, the human cloud, side hustles. No job? Pivot and retrain. Mired in debt? Plan better. Can't afford a home? Quit whining and move. We've seen, on the one hand, an *economic* transition from the welfare state to austerity and privatization, and on the other, a *cultural* transformation from community and shared obligations to individual liability.

This new discourse about work utterly blindsided labour. Its failure to recruit and organize young people who might have helped it respond and adjust was calamitous. The gig economy ravaged the taxi, hospitality, and tech industries, rendering them ripe for new levels of exploitation and abuse. Part-time, temporary, and contract work skyrocketed. Even unionized workers, especially in the public sector where union concentration is the highest, saw a sharp increase in temporary work: up 50 percent between 1997 and 2014.

Young Workers Fight Back

Unsurprisingly, it was young unionized workers who led the pushback between 2011 and 2014. Teaching assistants at multiple universities who went on strike in the middle of the decade emphasized student debt, housing costs, health benefits, and precarious contract employment. Young workers turned their back on Trudeau when he spoke at a CLC Young Workers' Conference in 2016, holding him to account for what they viewed as empty promises to youth—although they were chided at the time by senior labour leaders for their lack of "respectful dialogue." Unions might not have welcomed radical, young insurgency into their ranks, but it had found its way there nonetheless.

It was high time. The class war had crested in earnest—but not the war-on-the-rich narrative recited by our corporate stenographers. A 2015 report commissioned by the Canadian Centre for Policy Alternatives found that Canada's richest 10 percent doubled their wealth between 1999 and 2012. Canada's one hundred richest CEOs earned just under $9 million in compensation on average in 2014, while the average full-time worker in Canada earned $48,636. In fact, while young people struggled, four white guys named John made a staggering $114.9 million combined in 2014, far more than what five thousand full-time minimum wage workers would earn in a year.

Young people have watched time and time again as the big banks, stockbrokers, corporations, and fossil fuel multinationals get bailed out from crises caused by their own blind greed, reckless stupidity, or both. The oil and gas industry received an average of USD 2.74 billion in subsidies, and another USD 2.7 billion in loans each year during Harper's majority, despite a vacant promise in 2009 to phase out such giveaways. And to buttress his promilitary credentials, Harper promised $25 billion on F-35 stealth fighter jets while young people and other marginalized populations languished.

The money is there, you just can't have it. That's precarity's fickle calculus. How else can we account for the contradictory narratives we see on a daily basis in our media? Hit pieces on millennials run alongside reports of their bleak economic outlooks. Somehow, an entire generation is simultaneously both entitled and unemployed, spoiled and evicted, prodigal and hopelessly indebted.

In 2014, an anonymous group of radical leftists in Manchester, England, calling themselves the "Institute for Precarious Consciousness," published a manifesto of sorts titled "We Are All Very Anxious." They claim that anxiety is a "public secret." It's no longer simply a localized experience (say, around sex or public speaking), but an expansive field experienced throughout society that acts as the "linchpin of subordination" under contemporary capitalism.

For the Institute, anxiety isn't just a feeling or mental state *under* precarity—they're identical. Precarity and anxiety both render the possibility of social connection—with friends, family, a vocation, a community—

foreclosed: to drift in constant danger until you collapse and break down. This isn't just conjecture. An Ipsos poll in 2015 found that 52 percent of young people are at high risk of developing a major mental health issue, including depression. And while younger Canadians are more likely to be affected, depression and anxiety diagnoses are trending upwards across all demographics. The rates for previous generations, Boomers and Generation Xers, were far lower, at 14 and 35 percent respectively. A 2015 OECD study found that antidepressant use in Canada was among the highest in the world at eighty-five doses consumed each day per one thousand people.

We often think of precarity solely in terms of precarious work: low wages, no benefits, uncertain hours, informal relationships to employers, and minimal job security. But precarity is far more than financial insecurity. The psychological toll of living and working under precarity is wide-ranging and severe—it organizes and influences our social lives, it affects the way we plan for our future, and it exacerbates mental illness.

We now know that anxiety and precarity aren't some rough transitional phase of neoliberalism, but its resting states, both its consequences and the necessary conditions to survive it. The burnout, exhaustion, stress, and depression that are part and parcel of precarious capitalism aren't bugs in the system; they're features.

This is the backdrop of one of the most successful social movements in Canadian history: the momentous Quebec student strikes of 2012. In February of that year, students began protesting the provincial government's planned increases to postsecondary tuition. At one point, 310,000 of Quebec's 400,000 students were on strike. And it wasn't just the students, either: Quebecers from all walks of life banged their pots and pans in the streets in support of the students' brave stand against Jean Charest's intransigent Liberals.

Some observers dubbed it "Le Printemps Érable," a mildly appropriative pun on the Arab Spring protests roiling across North Africa and the Middle East at the same time. Charest's draconian Bill 78, an antiprotest law that contravened the Charter and earned condemnation from the United Nations, united Quebec behind the students' demands.

Most surprising were the lessons these hundreds of thousands of students and their allies learned on the streets. Students began by protesting a tuition increase that struck them as unfair and contrary to the principles of Quebec's national project. But when they earned the ire of the neoliberal state, the experience radicalized them. No longer a mere catalogue of complaints, the protests became a movement resisting neoliberalism itself, or, as the "Manifesto for a Maple Spring" puts it, a fight against the "laws of an unjust global economy that is mortgaging the future of all of us."

The students reached out to locked-out unionized workers, community organizers, and Indigenous groups and saw a common struggle. Students saw through Charest's transparent attempts to divide them and their movement; they refused. What began as a modest teenage protest had transformed into a crucible where a generation learned about the exploitative logic of capitalism and the vengeance of state power snubbed. Incredibly, against the odds, they brought down the Charest government.

This victory, however, would prove short-lived—and provide not the last evidence on how hollow electoral politics can sometimes crush what raw state coercion cannot. The students forced Charest to call a general election, and the movement, high on their extraordinary victory, disbanded. Quebec subsequently elected the Parti Québécois—who increased tuition by three percent in less than a year and to which bold, collective resistance was notably absent. The election, ironically, had defanged the unadulterated democracy of *le carré rouge*.

But the students had shown Quebec—and Canada—what democracy looks like. They had infected a generation of young people with the vocabulary of inequality and exposed the neoliberal project. They showed us that together, we can win. The Maple Spring imbued this education in Quebec's party of patient revolution, Quebec Solidaire, which learned that change does not come from elections, but first, always, from the ground. Eschewing the boom-and-bust strategy of electing charismatic leaders and hoping for traction, it continues to slowly build an ethos for the many, not for the few.

"Us versus Them"

If Harper's precarity program was bad for young people, it was downright criminal for migrants. For a country that prides itself on multiculturalism, Canada has a brutal record on how it treats those who come here seeking a safe place to live, work, and flourish.

Migrant labour built this country, from the Chinese workers who built the national railway to the temporary foreign workers who plow the fields and tend the crops that line supermarket shelves. For their contributions, Chinese Canadians paid in blood; their bodies line the Canadian Pacific Railway in the hundreds. They were forced to pay the racist Chinese Head Tax until 1923, when Chinese immigration was outlawed. Japanese Canadians had their homes stolen, their land and businesses expropriated, and their families imprisoned during the Second World War. The Komagata Maru arrived off the coast of Vancouver in 1914 with 376 Indian refugees, mostly Sikhs fleeing religious persecution. The ship was sequestered and ordered to return to India, where nearly all the passengers—those that survived the trip back—were arrested or murdered by British and Indian troops.

The Harper government continued this legacy, and they did it with pride. After securing their majority, Harper's Conservatives—led by then-Immigration Minister Jason Kenney—overhauled Canada's immigration law. Kenney introduced the infamous "four in, four out" rule, where migrant workers could work a maximum four years in Canada and then would be unable to return for four more years. Migrant labourers overwhelmingly work in the agriculture, construction, and child-care industries. Kenney's reforms put seventy thousand low-income migrant workers at immediate risk of deportation by 2015, the largest single deportation in Canadian history.

As the crises generated by neoliberalism proliferate and deepen, its architects need scapegoats to misdirect those affected. Harper et al. made over the race panics of yesteryear, dressing them up in the indifferent legislative language of federal policy. His precarity regime had laid fertile ground for a powerful and insidious logic of scarcity, of us vs. them. For the super-rich, there is endless wealth, endless tax breaks, endless bailouts;

for the rest of us, there are only this many jobs, that much public money—and the white public knew who to blame.

Kenney's laws epitomized the Conservatives' casual contempt for the labour that feeds Canadians, builds our infrastructure, and cares for our children—but nothing shows their cruelty like their record on migrant detention. During Harper's decade of rule, Canada imprisoned on average 11,000 migrants, sometimes indefinitely, including 807 children, every year. These practices continued under Prime Minister Trudeau. After a substantial drop in deportations and detentions following his election in 2015, his government ramped back up. The Liberal Government is building a brand new $38-million detention centre in Laval and has vowed to increase deportations by 25 to 35 percent each year.

Perhaps the ghastliest example of Harper's treatment of migrant workers was the case of forty-two-year-old Mexican refugee Lucía Vega Jiménez, an undocumented hotel worker in Vancouver. In December 2013, an armed transit cop overheard her accent and assumed she was not from Canada. He demanded proof of fare payment, which Jiménez could not provide. The Translink officer turned her over to the CBSA, who informed Jiménez that she would be deported—despite her insistence that she was fleeing domestic abuse, showing CBSA guards the scars from previous assaults. While the CBSA was processing her deportation, Jiménez hanged herself in her cell.

While this cruelty had immediate consequences for the migrant workers within our borders, the longer-term cost came in the vernacular of violence and division cultivated by the Conservatives and their supporters. Kenney is a master at sowing division. He has made a career out of knowing exactly where these fault lines lie and how to exploit them. He raised spectres of "anchor births," "bogus" claimants, and "security threats." He had the audacity to tweet out a celebration of the 2011 Cricket World Cup semi-final between India and Pakistan while 492 Sri Lankan Tamil refugees aboard the MV Sun Sea awaited deportation in Vancouver Harbour, a chilling echo of the Komagata Maru.

If Quebec's student movement gave Canadians the language and logic to fight neoliberalism, Harper's antimigrant program gave Canadians the language of fear and division. And this language is with us still. Kenney's successor Chris Alexander and eventual Conservative Party leadership candidate Kellie Leitch floated the idea of a "Barbaric Cultural Practices" hotline, where Canadians could snitch on their neighbours if they felt offended by difference. The tireless activists for migrant justice—at times undercut by their own allies—have fought this language for decades. They fight it now.

If border imperialism—to borrow Harsha Walia's phrase—teaches us anything, it is that the struggles of migrants and Indigenous people are linked under capitalism. One group can be marshalled by the powerful to stoke anger and frustration as easily as another. These borders create outsiders, some within our state, in the case of Indigenous nations, and some without, in the case of migrants displaced by the forces of global capital. These borders are fictitious at the best of times, but under precarity, they vacillate at the whim and fantasy of governments and multinational corporations.

Migrants and Indigenous peoples see these fictions for what they are. And they know how to fight them. The lessons we can learn from migrant justice activists and their Indigenous allies will not only teach us resilience in the face of despair; they represent the only strategy that can win.

Idle No More

Imperialism and colonialism are two of capitalism's greatest weapons. Colonialism seeks to separate Indigenous people from their source of strength and knowledge: the land. To resist this, Indigenous nations rely on an ethos of kinship and care—as verbs, not nouns—attending to a network of relations that extends far across space and time. It was a rare treat to see how Harper's neoliberal regime of division and chaos simply couldn't cope with the tender, patient, ironclad solidarity of Indigenous people in Canada.

Towards the end of 2012, three Indigenous women—Sylvia McAdam Saysewahum (Cree), Jessica Gordon (Pasqua First Nation), Nina Wilson (Nakota and Plains Cree)—and one non-Indigenous ally, Sheelah McLean, hosted a series of teach-ins in Saskatoon about the effect one of Harper's most notorious omnibus bills, Bill C-45, would have on Indigenous people. Bill C-45 was a devastating piece of legislation. It rewrote the Navigable Waters Act, eliminating almost all protections from water law and opening up Indigenous land to exploitation by resource and extraction industries. It made it easier for Canada to force First Nations to surrender reserve land for federal or industry use without Indigenous consent. It weakened the environmental review process and allowed corporations to opt out of environmental restoration commitments. And this didn't account for the litany of other abuses during Harper's tenure: underfunding educational commitments, shunning land claim negotiations, gutting Indigenous health funding and, most criminally, ignoring the thousands of Indigenous women, girls, and two-spirit people who have been murdered or gone missing in Canada.

McAdam, Gordon, Wilson, and McLean titled the Facebook page that scheduled these teach-ins "Idle No More" because they were tired of lawmakers taking their silence in the face of anti-Indigenous legislation, mistakenly or disingenuously, as consent. The spirit captured by that profound phrase, and the patient organizing work embodied by the teach-ins—in constant consultation with traditional Indigenous practices, elders and the knowledge embodied in the land—electrified anyone who heard it.

In December 2012, Attawapiskat Chief Theresa Spence went on a hunger strike to protest the deplorable conditions her people were forced to live under by Canada's neglect of its enshrined and fiduciary duty to provide basic services for the First Nations whose land it occupies. Her courage and perseverance as she waited, in vain, for a meeting with Prime Minister Harper to discuss his responsibilities for the poverty of her people became a powerful symbol of resilience and strength.

In January 2013, six young Cree from Whapmagoostui First Nation near James Bay walked 1,600 km to Ottawa to raise awareness of the poverty, lack of clean drinking water, and inadequate housing of Indigenous people in Canada. By the time "The Journey of the Nishiyuu"—"The Journey of the People"—arrived on Parliament Hill in March, their numbers had swelled to four hundred, and they were greeted by a crowd of thousands. Elizabeth May led a standing ovation in the House of

Commons, and NDP MP Romeo Saganash (Cree) and leader Thomas Mulcair referenced the Nishiyuu Walkers to raise Indigenous issues in Question Period.

One of my greatest ever pleasures as a staff member of rabble.ca was editing the work of Mi'kmaw lawyer, author, and warrior Pamela Palmater. I still miss the thrill of unleashing her fearless, singular voice on the milquetoast Canadian media landscape. Her writings on Idle No More during this momentous period remain essential. She describes a movement based on kinship with the land, kinship with all our relations near and far, kinship with our ancestors and the generations to come. "To me," Palmater writes,

> Idle No More is a responsibility – a responsibility to live up to the sacrifices of our ancestors, to the duty we have as guardians of the earth, and to the expectations that our children and grandchildren have of us to protect them. . . . I believe that we all carry that responsibility from the very moment the Creator blesses us with our first breath until our last.

The reverberations of Idle No More ring out still. Chief Spence never got her meeting with Harper; neither did the Nishiyuu Walkers. But they inserted Indigenous issues into the Canadian settler consciousness in a way that has never left. They would earn their Inquiry into Missing and Murdered Indigenous Women and Girls, albeit in a diluted and flawed form. Indigenous issues were a crucial pillar of the 2015 election that ousted Harper—although it was Justin Trudeau who would exploit Idle No More by promising a reformed "Nation-to-Nation" relationship, only to revert to the same colonial violence that built Canada.

But, just as Quebec students learned, revolutions are not won in elections alone. The women-led organizing power and belief earned in Idle No More would provide the foundation and blueprint for the movements that still drive us forward: the Wet'suwet'en resistance of 2019 and 2020 owes much to the four women who organized a small seminar on a piece of bad neoliberal legislation. The young writers and thinkers who emerged during Idle No More to call out colonial hypocrisy and lies are now major thought leaders and literary giants. Chelsea Vowell (Métis), whose *Indigenous Writes* is mandatory reading for any Indigenous Studies class, published her first writings during the Attawapiskat crisis. Billy-Ray Belcourt (Driftpile Cree) was a young queer Cree finishing up high school during Idle No More before he became a Griffin prize-winning poet and acclaimed essayist. Musicians including Tanya Tagaq (Inuk) and A Tribe Called Red released incendiary, provocative records during this time that provide soundscapes for contemporary Indigenous resistance.

Hope and Realism

It is impossible to comprehensively index the damage Harper unleashed on Canada's social fabric, and others have done a better job than I could hope. But to sketch a picture: antidemocratic omnibus bills became *de rigueur*, and Bill C-51 gave CSIS the right to spy on activists and Indigenous leaders; the Refugee Exclusion Act fast-tracked deportations of refugees from countries like Mexico and the Czech Republic, and migrant detentions skyrocketed; a series of once-in-a-lifetime policy changes decimated environmental protections, muzzled climate scientists, and, in some cases, actually ordered the destruction of government science library holdings; trade unions were subject to cumbersome and crippling reporting requirements and the drive to end Canada Post's door-to-door delivery undermined the country's most radical labour union, the CUPW; and, finally, Harper took aim at the constitutionally enshrined rights of Indigenous self-governance and did everything he could to separate Indigenous peoples from the land they had stewarded for thousands of years.

Perhaps the most devastating characteristic of Harper's ruthless program was the breathless pace at which it was accomplished. It left Canadians, particularly those most at risk and their allies, completely shellshocked: gutted, exhausted, vulnerable, and bereft of hope. Hope is often dismissed as an empty affectation in politics, but in truth, it is the most essential ingredient. Hope—not bland, uneducated hope, but hope built on purpose, intellect, and vision—is the lifeblood of a movement. If there is a better world out there—and there must be ("on a quiet day," Indian writer and activist Arundhati Roy assures us, "I can hear her breathing")—it will be hope that leads the way. The best organizers, the ones that build the scaffolding for our future out of the detritus of the present, never dwell on grief. They get to work.

The movements from the first half of the decade, movements forged in the crucible of anti-Harper activism, have proved invaluable. The most evident accomplishment of those years might also seem the most anti-climactic, however. Yes, Canada eventually managed to limit the brutal austerity of Stephen Harper's majority government to a single term, but this electoral victory, like many others, rang hollow.

In 2011, the New Democratic Party, buoyed by the charismatic leadership of Jack Layton, was enjoying an unprecedented surge. For the first time, something resembling social democracy appeared like a viable option in the face of the austerity consensus of Harper's Conservatives and the jaded Liberal Party of Paul Martin and Michael Ignatieff.

According to former rabble president and long-time columnist Duncan Cameron, the moment came in the popular Quebec talk show, *Tout le Monde en Parle*, when the respective leaders met to debate in front of a viewership of 1.5 million on April 3, 2011. Gilles Duceppe, one of the most popular politicians in Quebec history, confidently assured his base that only the Bloc Québécois could protect Québécois values from Harper's vicious conservatism. Jack Layton simply pointed to Harper, five years and three elections into his mandate, and looked directly at Duceppe. "*Il est encore là!*" Layton said. He is still there, Gilles. The election turned in a moment.

As Jesse McClaren points out in his snapshot of Canadian electoral history, the coming weeks changed the country forever. The strength of this surge was built upon the robust activism that had educated Canadians about the corporate giveaways in NAFTA and other emerging trade deals and Harper's increasingly antidemocratic audacity. (Who could forget the infamous "proroguing" of Parliament that almost—almost—resulted in a Liberal minority propped up by Layton's NDP).

It's hard to forget, even nine years later, the tragic irony of that 2011 election. As McClaren rightly points out, by most accounts, the Orange

Wave was a victory for the left: a historic NDP sweep in Quebec, a 12 percent increase nationwide in the popular vote, and a firm, pan-Canadian refusal of Ottawa's endless camaraderie with corporate interests.

It was a victory for the left by all accounts—all accounts but one. Most Canadians rejected Harper's mandate, rejected, as McLaren argues, corporate Canada, yet Harper managed to claim his long-sought majority through a meagre 2 percent increase in vote share—and the arcane caprice of our outdated first-past-the-post electoral system. That electoral glitch would cost Canadians deeply—and nine years later, the wounds have not healed. While the newly minted Official Opposition took over office space from bitter Liberal ex-MPs, activists, unionists, and organizers saw a dark storm coming. It's the blessing of the left to make predictions in the tea leaves of history and almost always find them proven correct; it's the curse that no one seems to listen before it's too late.

Less than four months after the election, Layton succumbed to cancer. His death, for his supporters, seemed to capture that mixture of excitement and loss: a celebration of a remarkable life in politics and an unprecedented win; and grief for the loss of a leader and a deep sense of foreboding of what was to come under a Harper majority.

On his deathbed, Layton reminded us, "Love is better than anger. Hope is better than fear. Optimism is better than despair. So let us be loving, hopeful and optimistic. And we'll change the world."

Tragically, the NDP would forget this powerful lesson. In 2015, Thomas Mulcair squandered the New Democrats' claim to the anti-Harper party by pursuing a strategy of aggressive respectability and conservatism. Mulcair had forgotten that Layton's popularity was girded by his support from social movements. He had forgotten that hope, not inoffensiveness, builds change. Indeed, even the polling lead the NDP enjoyed in early 2015 was a direct result of Mulcair's impressive coordination with the fight against Bill C-51. Yet, he would abandon it all for bland economic centrism and the elusive favour of Canada's right-wing press. It would fail spectacularly. A once-in-a-generation chance, wasted.

But far more crucial was the deep organizing and education work of Quebec's student movement, Idle No More, and migrant justice activists. For the first time, words like "neoliberalism" and "the 1%" began to enter our daily vernacular. The compassionate, brilliant work of migrant justice activists identified border imperialism as a critical node for understanding the ruthlessness of global capitalism, colonialism, and imperialism: an irreconcilable contradiction where goods can travel undisturbed across borders, but human lives cannot. Indigenous sovereignty and land rights became touchstones for a massive coming together across Turtle Island.

The reverberations of these movements would be part of the global generational shift we saw in the second half of the decade: one that stopped taking capitalist ideology for granted. Labour activists took on the gig economy, like the CUPW sensational win to organize delivery app workers for Foodora at the end of this decade. Younger demographics embraced socialist and social democratic policies by massive margins: universal pharmacare, dental care, support for Indigenous self-governance, a Green New Deal, and an end to masochistic dependencies on fossil fuels. Indigenous youth, led by women, queer, and two-spirit leaders are standing up to global capital and winning. They are leaning on their ancestors, on Idle No More, and they see another world is possible.

Cultural theorist Sara Ahmed argues that hope and anxiety share an intimacy. "In having hope we *become* anxious," she writes, "because hope involves wanting something that might or might not happen." Our younger generations seem to have that rare cocktail of hope and realism: raised with the belief that anything *ought* to be possible, but grounded in a real world where realizing that hope requires hard work, determination, and grit.

That world of possibility, of imagination—of hope—is not only possible, it's within our grasp.

2011 | Canada's Real Electoral Map: A Surge for the Left

Jesse McLaren

It's just a week after Canada's federal election, and the battle of interpretation is still raging. Some see a right-wing blue surge, others a dichotomy between Quebec and Canada, while the polls indicate a contradictory phenomenon. But looking at the shift between the NDP and the combined Conservative/Liberal vote, both long-term and between the last two elections, a different picture emerges—of an eroding but concentrated corporate vote and a surging NDP vote. This points to a left-wing shift in people's consciousness that creates possibilities for change if we can combine opposition inside Parliament with movements outside.

Harper's Optimism, People's Pessimism

One way of interpreting the recent election results is to only see a Harper majority, as if Canada were bathed in Conservative blue. Harper claims that Canadians voted for a "strong, stable, national Conservative government," and many agree. After all, the Conservatives did increase their seats from 143 to 167. People are anxious about what Harper could do with his majority—impose austerity, continue war and the tar sands, attack abortion rights and social services.

But assuming that Harper's majority signifies a right-wing surge in people's consciousness—as those on the right hope or those on the left despair—ignores the contradictions in the election and the possibilities for change. It's also true that a majority of people voted against Harper, and the Conservatives only increased their vote by 2 percent, so the picture must be more complex.

The Two Solitudes?

The most obvious challenge to Harper's claim is the historic surge of the NDP in Quebec, which halved the Tory and Liberal seats and decimated the Bloc Québécois. In the mainstream press, this has been interpreted as an isolated phenomenon connected to the rejection by people in Quebec of the quest for sovereignty. This analysis is wrong on both counts.

Firstly, the vote for the NDP in Quebec was not a vote against sovereignty but a shift to a party of the left. For twenty years, the Bloc Québécois has claimed the mantle of sovereignty but has delivered neither on this nor on important social reforms. Quebec has had the largest social movements—from antiwar protests to student strikes and labour mobilizations—and out of these has emerged a provincial left alternative, Québec solidaire, which links sovereignty to social justice issues. Years of anger against the Tories and the Liberals, the failure of the Bloc to deliver an alternative, the positive example of left sovereignty linked to mass movements, and an NDP campaign that included self-determination and opposition to the war in Afghanistan led people in Quebec to vote en masse for the NDP.

Secondly, while the NDP's biggest gains were in Quebec, they also picked up seats across the country—from BC to Ontario to New Brunswick. It's important for progressives in Quebec to know they have allies across Canada, and for people in English Canada to recognize the left-wing surge was not restricted to Quebec. Of 103 seats for the NDP,

58 come from Quebec and 45 from elsewhere in Canada. The electoral map is neither a sea of Tory blue nor a dichotomy between Quebec and Canada. Instead, the official NDP opposition in Parliament comes from across the country.

Erosion of the Corporate Vote under the Weight of Mass Movements

But the electoral map underrepresents the left-wing shift in people's consciousness. Firstly, it disconnects parties from their economic base, presenting them as abstract entities. As I've written elsewhere, the Liberals and the Tories are the twin parties of corporate Canada, who have both launched wars, undermined the environment, attacked civil liberties and social services, and imposed austerity. On the other hand, the NDP is the only party officially affiliated with labour and unofficially associated with social movements. Over the past ten years, the combined corporate vote has steadily declined, and the NDP vote increased—not because of what happened inside Parliament, but also because of what happened outside.

The two biggest gains for the NDP in the past ten years happened in 2004 (after the antiglobalization and antiwar protests of 2001–2003, when the NDP gained one million votes and increased their popular vote by 4 percent) and in this past election (after the economic crisis, mass protests in Wisconsin, and ongoing revolutions across North Africa and the Middle East, when the NDP gained two million votes and increased their popular vote by 12 percent). Over the past decade, these movements outside Parliament have depleted the combined corporate vote inside Parliament from 78 percent to 58 percent, a significant drop of 20 percent.

Shifting Consciousness between Elections

The second way in which the electoral map underrepresents shifting consciousness is that the first-past-the-post system shows who comes out on top but misses the dynamic of change underneath. The electoral map represents Parliamentary elections, but the main source of change happens between elections, driven by what happens outside Parliament. So to truly understand what has happened to people's consciousness between the past two elections, we need to look at the shift in votes. From 2008 to 2011, the NDP gained votes in 293 of 308 ridings, had the same vote in 10 ridings, and only lost votes in 5 ridings (one in Newfoundland & Labrador, three in Nova Scotia, and one in Ontario). This is better than any other party and shows that the "orange wave" was truly pan-Canadian. Not only did the NDP win 103 seats, but they came in second in more than 110 other ridings, including the ridings for Prime Minister Stephen Harper and Immigration Minister Jason Kenney, where the NDP gained about 2,500 votes in each, jumping from fourth place to second place (though still far away from winning).

Moreover, if we compare the votes for the NDP with the combined corporate vote, there was a net shift to the NDP in 216 ridings, or 70 percent. Even in the Tory stronghold of Alberta, there was a net shift towards the NDP in a quarter of the ridings (and an increase in votes in all but one riding). The resulting map is majority orange, not blue.

This surge to the left is missed if we only look at who won. In Quebec, Tory Maxime Bernier and Liberal Justin Trudeau held on to their seats, but the NDP tripled its vote in both ridings to surge into second place. In Ontario, Tory cabinet ministers Bev Oda and John Baird held on to their seats, but the NDP doubled its vote.

Looking at the shift in vote around Greater Toronto shows how Harper picked up so many seats to achieve his majority. In Etobicoke Centre and Ignatieff's riding of Etobicoke Lakeshore, the Liberals lost three thousand to four thousand votes to the Tories, but the NDP almost doubled its vote; in Scarborough Centre and Don Valley East, the Liberals lost five thousand votes, the Tories picked up two thousand to win, but the NDP picked up more than five thousand votes, doubling its share; in Bramalea-Gore-Malton the Liberals lost a third of their votes, the Tories gained one thousand votes, but the NDP picked up fourteen thousand votes, tripling its share.

In other words, the Harper majority is not based on a surge to the right, but a Liberal collapse. The corporate vote became concentrated in the Tories (who were endorsed by nearly every mainstream newspaper), while the real surge across the country was towards the NDP. This is an important step forward in quality as well as quantity. The aspirations of Quebec previously rooted in the corporate Bloc Québécois, the "strategic voting" for the corporate Liberals to stop the corporate Tories, and the isolated "neither left nor right" politics of the Green Party have shifted to a pan-Canadian labour party with links to the antiwar and other social movements.

Take the Surge to the Streets

But there is obvious asymmetry to this configuration. Harper has a majority in Parliament, but minority support outside Parliament. While it's to his advantage to reduce politics to what happens inside Parliament, his weakness can be exposed if the Opposition builds links to mass movements outside Parliament, especially the labour movement. In 2003 the Liberal majority wanted to join the war on Iraq and had the support of the opposition Tories. But the antiwar movement won the NDP to a principled antiwar position regardless of UN backing, and Jack Layton and the NDP helped build antiwar protests across the country—culminating in a trade union-led march of a quarter of a million in Montreal—which split the ruling Liberals and stopped them from joining the war.

This led to a surge in NDP support, which has since stagnated as the NDP leadership downplayed some of its most important policies—from ending the war in Afghanistan to stopping corporate tax cuts—while it contemplated a coalition with the Liberals. But with a shift in left-wing consciousness from global resistance to the economic crisis resulting in Liberal collapse and NDP surge, now is the time to put Harper on the defensive by raising all the demands of the movements: end the war, reverse the tax cuts, stop the tar sands, increase EI, and fund Medicare.

A decade of mobilizations has eroded the corporate vote, and inspiration from Cairo to Wisconsin has shifted people's consciousness to a left alternative—catapulting the NDP into Official Opposition. If we can continue building pan-Canadian mass movements and respect Quebec's right to self-determination, and if the NDP can unite with and help build these movements, we can expose how weak and unstable Harper's majority is and bring the change we all want.

Originally published on May 10, 2011.

2012 | Escalator to the Bottom: Quebec Students Refuse the Ride

Christopher Majka

With mammoth student protests in Montreal on May 22 (the *Globe and Mail* reported up to 250,000; CTV News reported 400,000), smaller protests in other parts of Quebec, and sympathetic marches in centres such as Calgary, Halifax, Toronto, Vancouver, New York and Paris, the attention of Canadians—and many across the globe—is turning to Quebec.

Trade unions are contributing to the province's student federations, and the Occupy Montreal movement has joined the protests. Both Montreal Mayor Gérald Tremblay and Parti Québécois leader Pauline Marois have said that the government must reopen negotiations. Fighting fire with petrol, Premier Jean Charest's government passed Bill 78, which contains a number of restrictive measures related to the protests and the student federations, thereby succeeding in inflaming passions further. A Léger Marketing poll found that 78 percent of Quebecers believe the government has gone too far with Bill 78, and 76 percent want the government to resume negotiations with the students. Lawyers for the student federations are preparing to challenge the constitutionality of Bill 78, which they feel violates freedoms of expression and association guaranteed by the Canadian Charter of Rights and Freedoms. The Quebec

Bar Association and the Quebec Human Rights Commission are equally concerned and have announced that they will investigate "all cases of discrimination" arising from the application of the law.

With all this attention has also come a flurry of criticism of the student federations. It's not my intention to survey or summarize them, but simply to dissect one current within the criticism to illustrate an underlying issue and how the critique is attempting to pigeonhole the student movement and its objectives into a form where it can be dismissed, or at least isolated. Margaret Wente's essay "Tuition Protesters Are the Greeks of Canada," published May 19, 2012, in the *Globe and Mail*, is one illustration. Wente fires several salvos in the direction of the protesters, but the central economic one which interests me is her contention that the Quebec socio-economic model "maxed out a while ago" and that the resistance to the tuition hikes (which Wente points out would still leave Quebec students with the lowest tuition rates in North America) stems from an "entitlement mentality." As a result, she claims, "the rest of Canada looks on, appalled."

Maxed Out Greed

Here's the problem with Wente's analysis: what has "maxed out" is actually greed. In the last generation, Canada's adjusted GDP has more than doubled, from $330 billion in 1980 to over $720 billion in 2009, an increase of 118 percent (adjusted for inflation, in constant 2009 USD; World Bank data). There is much more money in Canada today than there was thirty years ago. During this time, the Canadian population has increased 38 percent from 24.51 million to 33.89 million. So, Canada's adjusted GDP has grown 3.1 times faster than the population.

Therefore, things which were affordable in 1980 in Canadian society should be far more affordable today with so much extra wealth sloshing around in the country and only a modest increase in population. Are they? It seems not.

The median wage of Canadians has increased only 5.4 percent from about $45,800 in 1980 to $48,300 in 2009 (adjusted for inflation, in constant 2009 CAD; Statistics Canada). So, with per capita GDP having increased from $13,400 in 1980 to $21,300 in 2009, a 59 percent increase, while the median wage of Canadians has increased only 5.4 percent, where has all that money gone? Some to the rich, more to the richer, and most to the richest.

The income share of the top 20 percent (the top "quintile") of Canadians has increased from some 33.9 percent in 1990 to 41.7 percent in 2009. Even more revealing is the income growth of the richest 1 percent of Canadians. In a study entitled "The Rise of Canada's Richest 1%," economist Armine Yalnizyan of the Canadian Centre for Policy Alternatives found that while the income share of this richest group was 7.7 percent in 1977, by 2007, it had increased to 13.8 percent, almost doubling. Moreover, Yalnizyan writes,

> The data show the higher up the income ladder you climb, the faster the rise of the rich. The richest 1% has seen its share of total income double, the richest 0.1% has seen its share almost triple, and the richest 0.01% has seen its share more than *quintuple* since the late 1970s. Canada's elite are breaking new frontiers in income inequality.

If further empirical evidence was required, the Gini Index for Canada, a measure of income inequality, which was at 0.281 in 1989, has increased steadily to about 0.320 in 2009. The higher the index, the greater the income inequality.

These are the stark economic realities which underlie the student protests. While there is 59 percent more wealth per capita in Canadian society—implying that programs which benefit Canadians ought to command a higher level of support—this increased wealth is not reaching the working and middle classes whose financial prospects have largely flatlined over the past three decades at 5.4 percent. An ever-greater share of the pie is going to the rich, the very rich, and the über rich who are paying ever less tax. As Yalnizyan points out, in 1948, the top marginal tax rate in Canada was 80 percent; by 2009, it had dropped to 42.9 percent.

Furthermore, successive governments have cut rates of corporate taxation and sales tax, leaving more money in the pockets of corporations and the wealthy and less in the public purse to invest in programs such as postsecondary education. In the 1960s, the corporate tax rate in Canada was 40 percent; by 2000, it was 29.1 percent, and in 2012, it will become 15 percent, a decline of almost two-thirds in the span of the last fifty years. Over the last six years, the Harper Conservatives have decreased the Goods and Services Tax (GST) from 7 to 5 percent, a 30 percent decline in this revenue stream to the federal government.

The free-market, laissez-faire ideology of neo-conservatism has put the Canadian working and middle classes on a descending escalator to the bottom, their only remaining choice to try to slow the rate of descent. The Quebec student federations, however, beg to differ.

Beginning with the so-called "Quiet Revolution" of the 1960s when the provincial government took over control of the education system from the Catholic Church, significant investment in public education has become a centrepiece of Quebec society, which in turn transformed the province. Prior to that time, only 3 percent of Francophone Québécois and 11 percent of Anglophone Quebecers attended university. That proportion has subsequently increased to 38 percent at present as a result of the Quiet Revolution reforms.

How has this trickle-down poverty affected students? The Canadian Federation of Students says the average debt for university graduates is almost $27,000, and nearly two million Canadians have student loans that total over $20 billion. The weight of this debt burden has the potential to impoverish an entire generation of young people, who not only have to repay these substantial sums but are also doing so while paying an interest rate of between 5 and 9 percent. Here's a quick "back-of-the-napkin" calculation: in 2007–2008, there were 978,480 undergraduate and graduate students attending Canadian universities (Statistics Canada). The average undergraduate tuition in 2011–2012 is $5,366, and graduate tuition is $5,599 (for a total average of $5,482) (Statistics Canada). On this basis, Canadian students are paying about $5.364 billion every year in tuition.

Refusing the Ride

The Quebec student federations are posing important and legitimate questions about public investment in postsecondary education. Rather than being content to slow down the race to the bottom, they are asking whether we might instead consider changing the direction of the escalator. Rather than decreasing public investment in Quebec to bring tuition (and student debt) levels up to the Canadian mean, why not raise the bar—in both Quebec and the rest of Canada? The Canadian Council on Learning has shown that high quality, affordable, accessible, and flexible postsecondary education is essential to achieve Canada's economic and social objectives in the twenty-first century. Demand for skilful and knowledgeable workers in a variety of key professions and occupations is beginning to exceed supply, undermining Canada's productivity and competitiveness. Research and development (R&D) are key to economic success in a twenty-first-century knowledge-based economy, and Canada ranks fifteenth among the thirty OECD countries in R&D intensity.

So, in addition to removing an already crushing and escalating student debt burden that is limiting the degree to which students are able to pursue higher learning, decreasing or eliminating tuition is also highly advantageous for the social and economic strength of the country.

But, has the system of educational entitlements "maxed out" as Wente claims? Well, it depends on where your priorities lie. We know now that the Harper Conservatives propose to spend $25 billion on F-35 stealth fighter jets that are years behind schedule, whose costs continue to balloon, which are of dubious military utility to the Canadian Armed Forces, and which may be unable to patrol the Arctic (owing to the fact that they have a single engine, and even that is not included in the base price of the jets). Such a sum could wipe out all Canadian student debt with $5 billion left over. Or else $25 billion could be used to slash tuition by 50 percent for every Canadian student for an entire decade. Can we afford it? Certainly, if we can afford to contemplate purchasing F-35 stealth fighter jets. Imagine, however, how much more useful such an investment would be in education rather than in war machines. Is a desire for high quality, affordable, accessible, and flexible postsecondary education an "entitlement" as Wente claims? In that case, what about military entitlements? Do we want a well-educated, affluent population or expensive military toys for political boys? The choice is ours.

Originally published on May 24, 2012.

2013 | Idle No More: What Do We Want and Where Are We Headed?

Pamela Palmater

I have been honoured by the request of the Idle No More founders to be one of their organizers and spokespersons. Working within this movement was a natural extension of the work we already do in First Nations with leaders and citizens. In the last few weeks, many of the media's questions have related to how the movement started, what we want, and where it might be headed. I have done my best as one of the spokespeople to answer these questions based on the views shared with me by some of those in the movement.

I'd like to try to answer those questions as an individual. Thus what follows represents my own opinions, analysis, views, and aspirations about the Idle No More movement.

The Idle No More movement is part of a larger Indigenous movement that has been in the making for several years now. Indigenous activists all over the country have been monitoring the political and legal scene in Canada at both the federal and provincial levels and making a concerted effort to help inform First Nation community members and leaders about potential threats. We noted a clear assimilation agenda that emerged within the Conservative government, and we started planning how we could address that if Prime Minister Harper insisted on putting his plan into action.

We of course worked very hard to try all the usual channels to address our growing concerns, which included lobbying, letter-writing, testifying before Senate and Parliament, endless meetings with MPs, senators, ministers, and others—all to no avail. The Harper government was not interested in talking to us, let alone consulting us or getting our consent. Harper decided instead to use the Assembly of First Nations as his primary vehicle to call all the shots. Harper's government set the agenda, they drafted the joint action plans, and they alone decided what was and was not on the table. In other words, Harper managed to bully his assimilation plan onto the First Nation agenda with hardly a squeak of opposition at the political level.

At the co-called Crown-First Nation Gathering (CFNG) in January 2012, Harper promised First Nations his government would not unilaterally amend or repeal the Indian Act. After the CFNG, he broke that promise and proceeded with an aggressive legislative agenda that will include upwards of fourteen bills that will devastate our First Nations in various ways. It is the White Paper 2012 with a twist—instead of it being a policy, like the 1969 White Paper, which wanted to assimilate Indians, Harper's plan will be law. This is the spark that ignited the Idle No More movement into action.

We always knew action would be required at some point, but the legislation posed an imminent threat and required immediate mobilization. That is how a movement was born. In the early days, some were calling it the Idle No More movement, some calling it an Indigenous rights movement, but we all agreed that we needed to immediately oppose Harper's assimilatory legislative agenda. So many of the early activities included teach-ins, which helped explain the legislation's potential impacts on First Nations and, more importantly, what we could do to oppose it.

Early protests started out as opposing the massive omnibus Bill C-45 but later came to include the whole suite.

The Idle No More movement, initially started by women, is a peoples' movement that empowers Indigenous peoples to stand up for their Nations, lands, treaties, and sovereignty. This movement is unique because it is purposefully distanced from political and corporate influence. There is no elected leader, no paid executive director, and no bureaucracy or hierarchy that determines what any person or First Nation can and can't do. There are no colonial-based lines imposed on who joins the movement, thus issues around on and off-reserve, status and nonstatus, treaty and nontreaty, man or woman, elder or youth, chief or citizen do not come into play. This movement is inclusive of all our peoples.

To my mind, the true governing power of our Indigenous Nations has always been exercised through the voice of our peoples. The leaders were traditionally more like spokespeople who represented the views and decisions of the people. In this way, the Idle No More movement, led by grassroots peoples, connects very closely to our Indigenous traditional values. But it is not a movement where the people stand alone. Their elders, elected leaders, and traditional leaders stand with them. This movement is not in competition with any First Nation political organization or elected leaders. This movement is focused on the critical issues before us, not power struggles, political games, or competing for government funding. Everyone so far has donated their time, money, energy, and skills to make this work despite the inevitable critique, push-back, and misinformation.

Yet what makes this peoples' movement so unique is also what makes it so difficult for many Canadians and the media to understand. Generally speaking, people understand that each government, group, or organization has a leader, a clearly defined hierarchy, and rules about who can say and do what. This movement, on the other hand, is very organic and first and foremost respects the sovereignty of individual Indigenous peoples and their Nations to participate how and when they choose, if at all. This will mean that some First Nations leaders will choose not to participate, but some of their members will. It could mean one First Nation community organizes teach-ins, whereas First Nations peoples living in urban areas will get together and organize flash mob round dances.

Think of the many ways in which this movement has already developed. We had teach-ins at Louis Bull, Saddle Lake, and other First Nations. We have posted information, publications, and videos online for all to access. We have engaged the media to help educate the public about why this impacts them as well. The Chiefs organized a protest during the AFN assembly to oppose the legislation (including Bill C-45). Chief Spence is on a hunger strike standing up for all First Nations and the treaty relationship, which Canada has forgotten. Kids in schools have held Idle No More rallies, and there have been marches, protests, and temporary traffic and railway slowdowns. The core, unifying theme to all of it has been that they are peaceful activities meant to help educate Canadians about how this is in all our interest.

We do have structure, we are organized, we work very closely with one another across the country to strategize, and we are growing. We have worked with active First Nation leaders on the ground since the very beginning, and many of us continue to do so. Our allies increase every day as more and more organizations are joining the movement. Now we have widespread international support, which also grows every day. Pretty soon, you will see more and more prominent figures stand up to put pressure on Canada to come to the table in a real, meaningful way.

To me, Idle No More is a responsibility—a responsibility to live up to the sacrifices of our ancestors, to the duty we have as guardians of the earth, and to the expectations that our children and grandchildren have of us to protect them. Every single one of us has that responsibility, though, at any given time, we all have different capacities, skills, and opportunities in which to fulfil it. Regardless of our situation, I believe that we all carry that responsibility from the very moment the Creator blesses us with our first breath until our last.

This responsibility means that it is not good enough to work hard, get an education, find a job, and provide for one's family. These are important things, and our ancestors did their best to ensure that we would have a prosperous future. Many even negotiated these provisions in some of our treaties. But, it is not good enough for us to simply be comfortable, at least not as long as we have brothers, sisters, and community members who live without food, water, or housing. Right now, many of our Indigenous peoples are facing multiple, overlapping crises that require emergency attention. The very grassroots people standing on the front lines of this movement are there because they are the ones without clean water, housing, or sanitation, and the politicians have done little to address this.

This movement is set apart from any other before it. Unlike the Occupy movement, this movement involves peoples with shared histories, experiences, goals, and aspirations. We, as Indigenous peoples, are all related, we all care about each other's futures, and we share the same responsibility to protect our rights, cultures, and identities for our seventh generation. This movement also has a special spiritual significance in that this was prophesied—that the seventh generation would rise and restore the strength of our Nations, bring balance, and see that justice was restored to our peoples.

This movement is also unique in that it includes Canadians as our allies. Just as in the early days of contact when the settlers needed our help to survive the harsh winter months and seek out a new life here, Canadians once again need our help. They need our help to stop Harper's destructive environmental agenda. First Nations represent Canadians last, best hope at stopping Harper from the unfettered mass destruction of our shared lands, waters, plants, and animals in the name of resource development for export to foreign countries like China. Why? Because only First Nations have constitutionally protected Aboriginal and treaty rights, which mandate Canada to obtain the consent of First Nations prior to acting. These rights are also protected at the international level with the United Nations Declaration on the Rights of Indigenous Peoples.

When First Nations organize in Idle No More to oppose this legislation, they do so to protect all of our interests—First Nations and Canadian alike. The most precious resources in the near future will be farmable lands and drinkable water. If there is no clean water, it will impact everyone. We are standing up not only to protect our lands and waters but also to restore justice for First Nations and democracy for Canadians. We can work together to defeat this threat to Canada and find a way to share the lands and resources as the treaties envisioned.

The question of what we want can be answered in two parts. In the short term, Canada must withdraw the suite of legislation impacting First Nations, amend those omnibus bills that threaten our lands and waters, and restore the funding that was cut to our First Nation advocacy organizations and communities. In the long term, Canada must set up a nation-to-nation process whereby First Nations and Canada can address many of the long outstanding issues related to the implementation of treaties and sharing the lands and resources.

Ultimately, we want to be free to govern ourselves as we choose; free to enjoy our identities, cultures, languages, and traditions; free to live the good life as we see fit. This means Canada must respect our sovereignty and get out of the business of managing our lives. Given that Canada has worked hard to put us in the situation we are in, Harper will have to come to the table with some good faith and offer some solutions to address the current crisis facing many of our communities in relation to the basic essentials of life—water, sanitation, housing, and education. If Harper can do no more than appear at a meeting on January 24 as requested by the AFN, our most vulnerable citizens will not see justice.

What Idle No More means to me is the coming together of Indigenous peoples from all over Turtle Island to work together to restore pride in our peoples, stand up for our rights, and live up to those responsibilities we have to one another and Mother Earth.

It is inspiring hope when many had lost hope that anyone would ever stand on their behalf.

It has inspired pride in who we are as Indigenous peoples because our peoples and the ways of our peoples are beautiful and something to be cherished and defended.

It has inspired leadership in those who thought they had nothing left to offer their Nations.

It has inspired a reconnection of youth to elders, citizens to leaders, and men to stand beside their women.

It has inspired the most oppressed peoples to stand up and exercise their voices.

We are alive again, and the spirits of our ancestors are walking with us on this journey.

I believe in the power of our peoples—we can do this!

Originally published on January 4, 2013.

2014 | Four Reasons Why Shutting Down TFWP Is No Solution to Migrant Worker Abuse

Syed Hussan

There has been massive media attention on the Temporary Foreign Workers Program (TFWP) in the last few weeks. Mainstream and social media are full of analysis and solutions. Some critics and commentators insist that the only appropriate way forward is shutting down the low-skilled temporary foreign worker program. They are wrong.

With increased workplace uncertainty, as permanent jobs disappear and the public sector shrinks, many are looking around for culprits to blame. Though migrant workers and the TFWP seem like easy targets, they aren't.

It's important to analyze the key arguments being made about the TFWP.

Migrant Workers Are Pushing Canadians Out of Jobs and Taking Jobs from Unemployed Canadians

News outlets and commentators have reported how the total number of migrant workers entering the country make up one-quarter (some say three-quarters) of new jobs created in Canada, thus suggesting that migrant workers are taking jobs from young workers. The news media is full of a few cases where migrant workers are replacing citizen workers. This is missing the forest for the trees.

There were between 76,711 and 230,379 low-skilled migrant workers in Canada at the end of 2012—making them 0.0042 percent to 0.013 percent of the labour force (the large discrepancy between the figures is because 153,668 workers' occupational classification is not reported by Immigration Canada). Of these, about 35,000 worked in the agriculture sector, while another 19,830 were live-in caregivers.

There are officially 1.35 million unemployed Canadians in the country (real unemployment is likely twice as high). Even if all migrant workers were excluded, there would be at least 1.1 million unemployed Canadian citizens left. Communities with the highest levels of unemployment—like Nunavut—have relatively few migrant workers. The region with the lowest rate of unemployment—Alberta—has the highest number of migrant workers coming in. There is no generalized replacement of citizen workers by migrant workers. And it's well known that migrant workers are often replacing other migrant workers, like on southwestern Ontario farms where migrant workers have been coming since the mid-1960s.

Secondly, migrant workers are often coming into jobs that were previously also occupied by new immigrants. These are the low-paying jobs in gas stations, retail, and manufacturing that newcomers work in to get a leg-up. It's the same demographic of people—racialized, young, and middle-aged newcomers—who are working these jobs. Except now, they will be deported after a few years rather than build a life here. Immigrants have always formed a critical part of Canada's workforce. Only now, they are here temporarily.

There is absolutely no evidence that shutting out migrant workers would mean that employers would hire young Canadian citizens. That's because there is a major disconnect between labour, education, and training policy in the country. What is needed is government support for skills training, as well as income security—not migrant worker exclusion.

Employers and Corporations Are Using Migrant Workers to Keep Wages Low

The only reason migrant workers can be paid less and exploited more is because of two-tiered federal and provincial laws and legal limitations on collective organizing. In Ontario, for example, provincial law excludes many migrant workers from minimum wage, occupational health and safety guarantees, and even the landlord-tenancy act protections based on their occupational classifications.

Shutting down the TFWP would not mean that the employers would immediately raise wages for Canadian workers. Lobbyists for fast food restaurants like McDonald's, for example, have been advocating against minimum wage increases in Ontario. They might choose to move jobs to other regions in the world, advocate for more government subsidies and tax cuts, pass down increased costs to consumers, or do all of the above.

Many argue that migrant workers cause downward pressure on wages and work conditions; therefore, uplifting and empowering them is the only way to improve conditions for all.

Migrant Workers Are Less Likely to Stand Up against Abuse

Migrant workers are less likely to stand up to abuse because they have more to lose when speaking out. The real culprit here is the law that ties migrant workers to an employer and gives employers immense power to deport people at whim. The simple solution is full immigration status on landing, which would remove the coercive power employers and recruiters hold. It's also important to note that despite these limitations, migrant workers have organized, including mass rallies, speaking out against recruitment fees, fighting back against employer abuse, and more.

At a time when all the provinces are cutting resources from labour departments responsible for keeping corporations in check, abuse already encompasses citizen workers. It's not about abolishing the TFWP; it's about ensuring real labour protections for all.

Corporations Are Breaking the Law By Hiring Temporary Foreign Workers

Many have said that the temporary foreign worker program is being used illegally. That the TFWP is supposed to be a short-term labour shortage fix, and employers are making it otherwise. This is a profound misunderstanding of Canadian and global immigration policy.

Since 1978, more people have entered Canada on a temporary basis than on a permanent basis. This is not a new story, and there is no simple solution. Since Harper came into power in 2006, temporariness has been entrenched throughout the immigration system. It's not just that there are more temporary migrant workers; now parents, grandparents, and spouses also come in temporarily. Refugees and permanent residents face many different ways their status can be revoked—making them also temporary.

This is the new global face of immigration, with most "countries" expanding their guest worker programs, a regime that is being pushed at the United Nations level. The entire immigration system—not just the TFWP—is determined by corporate interests. The new expression of interest system is controlled by employers. Referred to as an "online dating" system, employers cherry-pick from immigrant applicants to fast-track who can come here permanently. Only workers from twenty-four occupations can apply.

Corporations aren't breaking the intent of the law. Temporary immigration is the law of Canada and the global norm. The solution is not to slam the door shut on migrant workers, or even, as some progressives insist, to simply expand the permanent immigration system. That would just mean more corporate-driven immigration. Poor and racialized workers (so-called "low-skilled workers") that make up the TFWP must be able to come to Canada freely with full immigration status on landing, including the ability to reunite with their families. We need to openly contest the factors that force people to move and create systems of migration that are people-driven, not corporate-driven. We need status for undocumented migrants now.

What Lies Beneath

Unlike stories of the deaths of migrant workers like Ned Peart, health care denial, racist policing, or mass exploitation like in the Presteve Case, it seems that only stories pitting migrants against "Canadians" get national attention. The use of incorrect statistics and skewed economic arguments to demand the exclusion of temporary foreign workers by people all along the political spectrum hearkens to a lengthy history of exclusion of immigrants from Canada. While in the past, racist headlines read "Immigrants Are Taking Canadian Jobs," now they insist "Foreign Workers Are Taking Canadian Jobs." What's the difference?

There is more afoot here. It's xenophobia, and it must be challenged. It is important that we do not repeat the injustices of the past. Full immigration status for all and full rights for all workers is the only way forward. Resist attempts to divide unemployed, migrant, and poor people.

Originally published on April 24, 2014.

2015–2020 | Section 4: No More Normal

Real Change Meets Radical Tactics

Nora Loreto

On July 3, 2016, the biggest event of Toronto Pride came to a halt. For thirty minutes, the honoured group Black Lives Matter-Toronto (BLM-TO) staged a sit-in full of theatrics at the annual Pride parade. There were costumes and capes, golden jewels stuck to cheeks, dramatic makeup, and a giant plume pen, chosen to be the instrument BLM-TO would ask the chair of Pride Toronto to use to sign his commitment to restore and protect Black and Afrocentric programming in the Pride agenda. And critically, to commit to refusing to allow uniformed police to march in the parade.

Prime Minister Justin Trudeau was also marching in the parade that day. Trudeau's staff, thinking that BLM-TO wanted to meet with him, offered a meeting right away. They declined: this one wasn't about him. The snub was a small but mighty indication that BLM-TO had achieved a level of notoriety and confidence rare among progressive groups. Black Lives Matter defined and redefined activism in the latter half of the 2010s. The movement showed Canadians how to protest in the twenty-first century: deploying old tactics like road blockades, occupations, and rallies, while leveraging social media to amplify their message. At a time when the left felt unable to harness collective action to demand changes from politicians or corporations, BLM-TO formed a movement that created space for relationships to grow, art to flourish, and consensus to stem from intense debates and discussion.

By July 2016, Trudeau had only been in power a short while, and he had ridden a wave of progressive promises that he had not yet abandoned. Photos of Trudeau at Pride wearing a big smile and a pink shirt with the top buttons undone were about as different as a white man could look from Stephen Harper. Trudeau's image would later crumble: his enthusiasm for costumes would get him into trouble during his 2019 reelection campaign when it was revealed he had donned Blackface some number of times (three at least, maybe more, he admitted), and his progressive persona would fall apart when it became clear that his left-wing promises would never go further than campaign slogans. In the latter half of the 2010s, the veneer of the Liberal Party would finally start to fall away, and in the Liberals' quest to maintain the status quo, thousands of Canadians would find themselves disenfranchised, frustrated, and disappointed by the world's darling feminist Prime Minister.

In the same period, the left started to renew itself, both by going back to classic tactics that disrupt and bother the status quo and also by experimenting with new forms of civil disobedience. Unlike the Harper era, progressives finally had an opening to push the government to enact more progressive social policy. Trudeau was a welcome change from the nine years under Harper's rule. It soon became clear that Trudeau's promise of "real change" had melted into minor change, and that Harper's status quo would remain firmly entrenched.

In response to this betrayal, activists found new ways to fight back: Black Lives Matter used a diversity of tactics to force politicians and the media to pay attention to anti-Black racism. But they were far from the only ones experimenting with different tactics and pushing demands that posed a direct confrontation to power. Indigenous activists used land occupation and reclamation to physically block pipeline development, and when the traditional leadership of the Wet'suwet'en people called for solidarity actions in early 2020, rail corridors across Canada were blocked, and marches and sit-ins slowed traffic. It coincided with an emergent environmental movement that was young, radical, and prepared to engage in civil disobedience in the face of a government whose greenwashed policies could not stand up against their industry-friendly subsidies or the purchase of a gas pipeline. There was also a renewed energy and activism around feminism that rose up in reaction to the hollow words of Justin Trudeau and his feminist decrees, and as mainstream consciousness among feminists that white, bourgeois feminism is not only not enough for women, but also actively hurts nonwhite women, nonbinary people, disabled, trans, and poor women. The thread that tied all activism together was the slow but certain death of liberalism, expressed in the Liberal Party of Canada and Trudeau himself, with whom trade agreements could be feminist, pipelines could be reconciliation, and anti-Black racism could be undone by a guy who said he couldn't remember how many times he had worn Blackface.

Electoral Reform

The day after Justin Trudeau was elected Prime Minister, rabble.ca's federal politics reporter Karl Nerenberg zeroed in on the most significant challenge Trudeau faced: would Canada's new prime minister keep the many and significant promises he made to win the election? Trudeau's most ambitious promise was undoubtedly electoral reform. Electoral reform enticed a good number of progressive voters to cast a so-called "strategic vote" for Trudeau's Liberals so long as this would be the final election held under the first-past-the-post system. Electoral reform was a symbolic promise. Like Trudeau's social justice image, it was a mirage meant to siphon away votes from the NDP, and people believed it.

Electoral reform was a promise that didn't appear out of thin air: progressive organizations had campaigned for years for the electoral system to change. After they were elected, the Liberals established a commission to study electoral reform. Organizations and individuals attended, made deputations, and laid the groundwork for a general consensus to arise: the best alternative system was Mixed-Member Proportional (MMP). Under MMP, electors are given two votes: one that elects a local MP, similar to the current system, first-past-the-post, and a second that allows voters to choose which party they prefer.

MMP is used by liberal democracies around the world but would near certainly ensure that the majoritarian rule of the Conservatives and the Liberals would become a fossil of an older system: one where parties are rewarded with full and unchecked parliamentary power even if their majority was earned by votes from just one-quarter of the population. The cynics—who warned that the Liberals would never overhaul our electoral system—were right. In 2017, Trudeau backtracked on his campaign promise from 2015. There was no way that the Liberal Party, a party that has always benefited from false majorities produced by our current system, would adopt a new system, and certainly not one that favours minority governments with more parties represented by fewer seats, which would have been the case under MMP.

Reforming Canada's voting system would have been the most significant change to our parliamentary democracy since the country was founded in 1867, more significant than universal suffrage or repatriating the constitution. Liberal democracy requires that the population has hope that things are getting better. In return for popular support, liberal democracy is supposed to offer people services to help them in times of need: public education, public health care, civic services, roads, mail, and other important infrastructure. But after three decades of austerity under both Liberal and Conservative governments, Canada's public services are hollowed out or, worse, privatized, and our welfare state greatly eroded. This has seeded a level of disenfranchisement that has kept young people away from voting and makes average voters extremely sceptical of the promises made by politicians.

Shutting It Down

In April 2016, Black Lives Matter-Toronto activists staged an occupation of the Toronto police headquarters. They were frustrated by the lack of justice and transparency around SIU investigations of the police murders of two Black men: Andrew Loku and Jermaine Carby. The occupation lasted for two weeks, and the encampment outside the headquarters became a location where people could come and share a meal, learn a new skill, sing, dance, or simply sit around a fire together, keeping warm on the concrete.

The action forced politicians and journalists to pay attention to the ways in which anti-Black racism is manifest in Ontario, especially in policing. During their campaign, a right-wing radio personality wrote a hit piece smearing Yusra Khogali, a co-founder of BLM-TO. As a result, Khogali was harassed, threatened, and targeted. When a CP24 reporter tried to interview another BLM-TO co-founder, Sandy Hudson, about it, Hudson refused, asking the reporter the simple question: "Why are you doing this story?" to challenge the legitimacy of the manufactured story. On rabble, Mark Brown, a postal worker and member of the Coalition of Black Trade Unionists, wrote about this exchange, arguing that BLM-TO's capacity to confront power, both journalists and politicians, would go down as an important example of Black resistance.

BLM-TO mastered a diversity of tactics. Activists engaged on every plane: through mainstream media, but also by telling their own stories online and in various books; through protest tactics, like blocking a highway and occupying space; and through creative actions, like the famous one at Toronto Pride. Activists from BLM-TO created the Freedom School, Afrocentric educational programming for children in a Black-positive, queer, and disabled-integrated space. BLM-TO created art and dance and opened a space where performances and displays could be organized. They exposed anti-Black racism in Canada so that no one could publicly deny that racism towards Black people is differently pernicious and harmful. They showed activists across the country that all social movements must be broad-based and bring together people of all ages and genders, talents and perspectives, united by a single cause.

Organizing an occupation is not easy. A successful occupation requires intense commitment, lots of co-ordination, and dedication from both the occupiers and their supporters. While the Occupy movement had helped to mainstream the tactic years prior, that movement fell apart in too many locations where occupations became complicated operations, often in public parks that made them easy to break up. The BLM-TO occupation of Toronto police headquarters in 2016 turned into a two-week expression of community-making.

But BLM-TO was not the only group that organized effective and successful occupations during this period. So too did the Tiny House Movement, which saw Indigenous land defenders and activists physically block pipeline construction on unceded Indigenous land along Canada's west coast—notably the Trans Mountain Pipeline expansion project—by building and occupying tiny wooden houses.

The Trans Mountain Pipeline expansion project, initiated by Kinder Morgan, is promised to triple the capacity of an existing pipeline—to nine hundred thousand barrels per day—by building almost one thousand kilometres of new pipeline between Edmonton and Burnaby. The project faced a formidable opponent in the Tiny House Movement: Indigenous people whose physical presence along the 518 kilometres of unceded Secwepemc territory slowed and attempted to halt the construction of the pipeline. Tiny House Warriors built small housing structures along the proposed pipeline's path to try to stop the project and protect the land the pipeline passes through and the surrounding water basins.

In her 2017 story "Tiny Houses, Enormous Statement," Erin Despard argues that the tiny houses served as a reminder of the deep connection that persists between physical dwellings and the land we occupy. The houses stood as symbols of homeland to assert that pipeline projects pass through unceded land, but also as physical shelters—locations where people could live off the grid in a sustainable way. This combination of symbolism and practicality was powerful, showing both the need for Indigenous people and their communities to assert their right to sovereignty over traditional territory and to physically take back space from corporations and the Canadian state.

Creating community is a radical act in the face of neoliberal economic policy, and tiny houses were not only used at the Secwepemc blockade. Wet'suwet'en leaders and allies also built small homes and buildings along the proposed path for the Coastal GasLink pipeline. By building physical homes that could be lived in and powered without needing to be connected to the grid, these activists successfully combined many issues into one impressive resistance: housing as a human right, Indigenous sovereignty and connection to land, occupying space as a means to confront power, and living in ways that don't rely on destructive or dirty energies.

Despard argues that the Tiny House Warriors' action could offer a path forward for collective and communal approaches to land management and food production. And as the coronavirus pandemic has laid bare, resisting and surviving by relying on locally grown and tended food systems might be the only way to ensure that we can survive in a post-globalization era. This includes respecting Indigenous law and Indigenous communities' right to say no to Canadian resource extraction projects.

In 2018, the Trudeau government bought the Trans Mountain pipeline from Kinder Morgan for at least $12 billion, though the price keeps increasing as construction costs balloon. (It is increasingly difficult to imagine the government will find a buyer for this massive purchase.) One year after the purchase, the federal Liberals approved the project—the government had purchased the pipeline before it passed through the regulatory hoops necessary to even obtain Parliament's approval. The Tiny House Warriors promised to continue to resist the pipeline. In a press release issued on the day the project was approved, activist Kanahus Manuel said, "To try to legitimize this illegal act, Canada uses what legal scholars call its 'cunning misinterpretation of "consent"' which is inconsistent with Indigenous, constitutional and international law."

Building houses along pipeline pathways was just one of many tactics used to resist resource extraction over the past five years. Some climate justice activists took a more direct, almost too-obvious approach to activism: they simply turned off several pipelines. In one case, American activists closed a pipeline that carried Alberta crude to refineries in the United States. Shutting down a pipeline, much like blocking traffic or blockading railways, is nonviolent direct action that momentarily stops production. Any slowdown, whether through turning a valve or blocking a railway, sends the message that people are so opposed to resource extraction infrastructure that they will risk hefty fines and jail time just to turn off the taps. These actions threaten the shipment of oil and threaten profits, cutting to the heart of the extractivist economies that uphold the colonial projects of both Canada and the United States.

Climate activists and Indigenous land defenders know that our window for curbing climate breakdown has narrowed drastically in the past five years. While political leaders equivocate on climate policy and embrace market-based solutions like a carbon tax, direct action to slow or even stop industry has become ever more urgent. Whether by building housing along a proposed pipeline, turning off valves for a few hours, or shutting down Canada's entire rail network, every single action pushes us closer to viable alternatives and makes it increasingly hard for industry to justify dirty, expensive, and risky resource extraction projects.

New Kinds of Old Organizing

The final years of the 2010s also witnessed a resurgence in feminist action. But unlike other movements, feminists have not figured out how to regroup, reorient, and reorganize. From 2015 to 2019, social media became the most popular location to stage feminist actions. Feminists talked about times that they had #BeenRapedNeverReported or, through the hashtag #MeToo, how they had also experienced sexual assault. Viral hashtags took aim at violence against women and gave feminists a virtual outlet to talk about their experiences of gendered violence. People were able to shout their abortions (#ShoutYourAbortion), call out abusers or take back their agency, and talk about their experiences. But unlike Black Lives Matter and Indigenous-led climate justice movements, online feminist activism rarely exited the online world to create a Main Street confrontation, especially in Canada. Instead, the most important feminist action was confined to front-line services, in shelters and abortion clinics, where activists are too overwhelmed with demand to be able to organize new pan-Canadian forms of feminist action. And so, much feminist activism has lived online.

The feminist movement is also not like other movements. Effective Black and Indigenous movements for liberation and civil rights have a clear understanding of power and white supremacy. Their confrontations seek to undermine this power, expose hypocrisy, and convince onlookers to understand issues through a decolonial or antiracist frame. Climate justice movements have also managed to move away from the mainstream, white-dominant spaces of the sustainability movement, to become a far more diverse group of activists who take direct action to challenge the status quo. There's been no similar change with feminism. For what remains of the mainstream feminist movement, the dominant frame is still firmly white. Whiteness obscures the fact that women do not experience systemic violence in the same way. It creates a tent so large that feminism becomes a matter of self-identity: either you're a feminist, or you hate women.

As a result, feminism has become slippery and toothless. When Prime Minister Justin Trudeau declared that he would be a feminist prime minister, there was barely a chorus of feminists ready to ridicule such a hilarious promise. Instead, the press ran with the label, and he was able to call himself feminist with few challenges for the first years of his mandate. But Canadians have countless examples of how Trudeau's brand of feminism, like his shallow positions on all progressive issues, has ignored the most marginalized women. As prime minister, Trudeau failed to put sufficient measures in place for parents to access child care, despite his campaign promise that the universal child care benefit would help secure child care for all who need it. When his government announced the Canada Emergency Response Benefit (CERB) in response to the coronavirus pandemic in March 2020, they disqualified everyone who made less than $5,000 in 2019 and threatened jail for anyone who "abused" the system. This means-tested policy had a particularly pernicious impact on marginalized women and was a good example of the brand of feminism that the federal Liberals prefer: a feminism that fights for minor gains for women who are already privileged.

When it comes to significant feminist issues, like abortion, Canadians have been told that we have it good. We're told that abortion isn't under threat in Canada, especially if we compare ourselves to the United States, where, over the course of the 2010s, lawmakers in conservative states passed a wave of policies that restricted individuals' right to choose an abortion. In her 2019 article for rabble, "The War on Women is Still On," Antonia Zerbisias issued a serious warning for Canadian feminists, arguing that insufficient child care, a stubborn pay equity gap, and the connections between Alberta Premier Jason Kenney and the anti-abortion movement in Alberta are proof that there is a war on women—albeit a stealthier one—raging in Canada, too. Zerbisias is right to sound this alarm. Conservative movements across Canada that want to gut women's rights for both ideological and fiscal reasons are on the rise. From the Campaign Life Coalition to anti-choice activists who have entered mainstream politics, these movements are well funded and have demonstrated that they can impact political decision-making.

Women's access to abortion services in Canada remains under threat. That threat isn't like it is in the United States, where increasingly restrictive pieces of legislation are co-ordinated to pass in antiwomen legislatures. Instead, our right to abortion is threatened by severe underfunding, such that people lose access to the full range of reproductive health services: from abortion to prenatal care, from hospital care to postpartum. While Trudeau's Liberals have affirmed and reaffirmed their pro-choice position, the government was not able to ensure that New Brunswick's only abortion clinic stayed open, as it risked closing in 2020 due to a lack of funds. When a health system has its funding regularly cut—as our systems have over the past thirty years—the impact disproportionately hurts reproductive care. This underfunding became acute when the coronavirus hit our health care system, shutting large sections of the system so that all resources and forces available could be marshalled towards fighting the pandemic.

So much of Trudeau's feminist brand has depended on invoking a boogeyman: first, Stephen Harper, and later, Donald Trump. But as Trudeau took office for his second mandate, having failed to deliver on key feminist policies like universal child care or home care, it became clear that, in the policy arena, Canadians could expect more of the same. And, with a minority government elected in 2019, the feminist zeal with which he rode into the PMO was noticeably tempered. Maybe internal polling suggested they lay off the feminist label a little?

Pandemic Politics

The news that much of the world would spend much of 2020 locked in their homes, only leaving to work in essential services or to buy groceries, was the consumption curveball that few predicted. The pandemic changed everything. It stopped society in its tracks. It plunged the stock market into record lows. It took the lives of hundreds of thousands of people. It laid bare a truth that many have activists have said all along: that our way of life is not just. It has shown us that everything can be transformed.

In the initial chaos of the pandemic, Canada and the provinces took precautions that may have seemed extreme at the start, but that would help contain the virus to the extent that was possible. The Liberals were first hailed for their steady hand and transparent communications. But, when the vote needed to happen on the relief funding that they had promised for Canadians, they slipped in language that would give their caucus the power over spending and taxation until 2021. Opposition parties moved quickly to insist that these parts of the legislation be removed, and they were.

The Liberals' attempted power grab is no surprise. The Liberals are a party of money and business, and they would be happy to dispense with pesky parliamentary oversight if only to allow them to pass whatever legislation they would like. By trying to sneak in this extraordinary power, the Liberals had hoped that the chaos of the current moment, combined with Canadians' need for financial relief, would have allowed them to force the bill through as it was.

It was a dire warning: politicians have always been willing, if not eager, to ditch democratic oversight in a time of crisis. The coronavirus crisis has exposed capitalism for what it is: vicious and brutal, with little care for the people that it hurts or kills. Many people in Canada threatened to withhold rent and demanded that frontline workers—from grocery clerks to truck drivers—receive hazard pay. As Canada's health care systems falter, as we reckon with the reality that a profit-driven economy is a death sentence, more and more people are developing a shared understanding that there is no "returning to normal." The pandemic has made it clear that everything must change.

As Canada emerged from the first phase of the pandemic, there was a clear fight between those who want to protect and maintain the status quo and those who want the world to change. The incredible mass protests that unfolded in May and June of 2020, even while gathering in public together was supposed to be prohibited, showed the spirit and determination that exists for things to change: for police departments to be dismantled, for anti-Black racism to be rooted out of society, and for a new world to emerge that is more just.

But corporate CEOs and powerful special interests are busy making the same calculation: what can be cut even further, which corporations will see the largest bailouts, who will make money off this crisis, and how the wealthy and powerful will establish a new "normal" that is even more brutal than the previous status quo. The struggle between these two poles is going to underpin all social movement struggles in the next several years. What started in May 2020 and spread across Canada will only survive if organizers can orient their movements towards power: to identify what levers they can pull to force politics, businesses, and media to change. Marches on their own are not enough.

The Way Ahead

Progressive movements untethered from partisan politics showed us that the only way to make progressive social change is through movement building: strategic campaigns and demands buoyed by radical tactics. Indigenous and Black civil rights movements achieved this where the feminist movement wasn't able to. Corporate bourgeois feminism has confused a lot of progressive activists, who think that maybe feminist victory can be found in the election of a feminist Liberal government. But feminism, the kind that fights for the liberation of all women and nonbinary folks, and not just white women, must be accompanied by struggles against colonialism and white supremacy. Feminists need to shed respectability politics and build our fight in the streets (and along pipeline routes, and at police headquarters). Anything short of this will get co-opted by corporate interests, or it simply won't be enough.

If the early 2010s were a period where repression and draconian laws were Canada's norm, the second half of the decade showed that people living across Turtle Island, both Indigenous and settlers, could organize themselves to restore community power and push back against neoliberal politics and policies. During this period, Canada's corporate-owned mainstream media consolidated further, and the power of social media platforms to shape our every interaction online became impossible to ignore, prompting the activists organizing to build movement infrastructure and popular support around progressive principles and policies to wrestle with complex questions about the effectiveness of digital tactics. The limit of digital activism was starting to become undeniable: during every flash-point event, the digital world would be flooded with corporate advertising masked as a solidarity statement, while social media left activists open to harassment and surveillance. The new activism that emerged blended digital and real-life tactics, leaning hard on the latter, while using the former to signal boost, make connections, raise money, and offer a direct path to witness resistance and injustice. The groundwork and vision forged by social movement activists in the years following Trudeau's election offer a clear path out of the crisis that stopped everything in 2020.

2015 | Prime Minister-Designate Justin Trudeau Has Many Promises to Keep

Karl Nerenberg

After one of his three majority victories, Pierre Elliott Trudeau quoted a line from New Hampshire poet Robert Frost's "Stopping by the Woods on a Snowy Evening": "I have promises to keep / And miles to go before I sleep."

At the late prime minister's funeral in 2000, his eldest son Justin paraphrased that quote:

"He kept his promises and earned his sleep."

It is Justin Trudeau who now has promises to keep. He made many, many promises during this campaign, possibly more than his father made in his five election campaigns combined. Here are just sixteen of them:

1. To create a special, all-party parliamentary committee to study alternatives to the current first-past-the-post electoral system, and, within eighteen months, introduce legislation to replace first-past-the-post, based on the committee's recommendations. That is a key promise, and one that the power brokers and insiders of the Liberal party will not want the new prime minister to keep.

It will take determination and fortitude on Justin Trudeau's part to resist the many who will advise him to shelve that particular pledge.

The cynics are already saying we can forget about electoral reform. On election night, when one member of a Radio-Canada panel evoked that particular Trudeau pledge, there were snickers all around. When has it ever happened, the panellists said, almost with one voice, that a party wins a majority under one voting system and turns around and changes that system?

Those who voted for the Liberals with hearts full of hope—especially those who said theirs was a strategic vote necessitated by our unfair and unrepresentative electoral system—might want to start actively encouraging their party of choice to honour this particular promise. If enacted, electoral reform would change the face of Canadian democracy for generations to come. It would be a true and lasting legacy project for Justin Trudeau's new government.

2. To get the Canada Revenue Agency to proactively inform Canadians who have failed to apply for benefits of their right to do so; and, more important, to end the Harper government's politically motivated harassment of charities.
3. To restore home delivery of mail.
4. To extend the federal access to information law to the prime minister's and cabinet ministers' offices.
5. To institute parliamentary oversight of Canada's security agencies, involving all parties in the House.
6. To appoint a commissioner to assure that all government advertising is nonpartisan.
7. To end the odious and antiparliamentary practice of stuffing disparate pieces of legislation into massive omnibus bills. This was a trademark of the Stephen Harper regime.
8. To have all Parliamentary committee chairs elected by the full House, by secret ballot. Currently, committee chairs are purely partisan appointments of the Prime Minister.
9. To end Stephen Harper's war on science and restore the compulsory long-form census.
10. To name an equal number of women and men to the cabinet.

Those are just some of the many Liberal promises that relate to democratic reform. Justin Trudeau announced those reform commitments, and a number of others—with much fanfare—this past June. Trudeau's newly elected Liberal party has also promised:

11. To restore health care for refugees and reinstitute family reunification in immigration. They would allow, for instance, elderly parents to join their families in Canada as permanent residents, entitled to health care and other services. The Harper government has consigned such folks to precarious status on annually renewable visitor visas.
12. To make a major investment in on-reserve First Nations education, without imposing Harper's humiliating and draconian conditions on First Nations communities, all in the context of a renewed nation-to-nation relationship with Canada's First Nations, Inuit, and Métis people.
13. To find a consensus with the provinces to achieve real progress on greenhouse gas reductions. Notably, Trudeau has not yet set any emission reduction targets for Canada. But he has long described himself as an environmentalist and says he is committed to seeing Canada take a leadership role in the fight against climate change. Canadians who worry about global warming might want to watch carefully how the new government performs on this file. The UN Conference of the Parties on climate change will start in just over a month, in Paris.
14. To restore funding for CBC/Radio-Canada. The Liberal record on this—going back to the Jean Chrétien and Paul Martin days—is not encouraging. But Montreal MP and former leader Stéphane Dion has taken a strong, well-articulated, and committed position on this dossier. And one hopes the new government will recognize that federal support for public broadcasting involves more than the CBC alone. It must also include the National Film Board, Telefilm Canada, and the full range of federal funding mechanisms for the production and distribution of programs and films that tell Canada's story.
15. To end Canada's participation in bombing raids on Iraq and Syria.

And finally:

16. To bring twenty-five thousand Syrian refugees to Canada by the end of this year.

It is a big and ambitious agenda. And, of course, the list is far from exhaustive.

Those who voted for this new government were ready to put aside thoughts of Liberal scandals of the past. On Monday October 19, and at the advanced polls earlier, the legions of Liberal voters, many of whom had voted for Jack Layton's NDP last time, were not thinking of the insiders and lobbyists who swarmed around previous Liberal governments. Mostly, one suspects, they wanted to drive a stake through the heart of the loathsome Harper regime. A great many voters did not want to risk an uncertain result. They were ready to put their unqualified faith in the optimism, energy, and hope of the young Liberal leader—now the next prime minister.

Bubbly, Enthusiastic, Energetic, Almost Preternaturally Cheerful

As for Justin Trudeau, the person and leader, I first met him in 2009 when he was a newly elected MP. At the time, I was doing policy work for an advocacy organization called Volunteer Canada. Trudeau had a private member's bill before the House that related to volunteering, and when I heard about it, I called Trudeau's aide, smart and capable Louis Alexandre Lanthier, who had previously worked for Liberal MP Ken Dryden.

Lanthier invited me to lunch in the sixth floor Parliamentary Dining Room to talk things over, and I expected to be talking only to him. But when the time came, Trudeau himself appeared. He was pretty much the same in private as in public: bubbly, enthusiastic, energetic, almost preternaturally cheerful.

I was in the visitors' gallery when Trudeau gave his first speech in the House, in support of his own bill. It was a sleepy evening in February, and the place was largely empty. One NDP MP did rise to his feet to support the young Liberal MP and spoke admiringly about Trudeau's late father.

Justin Trudeau and I met a few more times on the volunteering issue, but I was more impressed with Trudeau's policy acumen when I met him, about a year later, to, in effect, lobby on behalf of beleaguered Roma refugees from Central Europe, whom the Harper government had decided to demonize as "bogus" and "queue jumpers." I had a different view as a result of a documentary film I was directing on the Canadian Roma, *Never Come Back*.

At the time, the cautious and by nature small-c conservative Michael Ignatieff was Liberal leader, and Trudeau was the party's immigration critic. In that capacity, he knew his stuff. In fact, he educated me about some of the principles of refugee policy.

I asked him how one would counter the Harper government argument that Roma couldn't be refugees because they came from "safe," liberal-democratic European countries. Trudeau explained that there is something called the duty to protect. Even if governments in such countries as Hungary do not actively persecute the Roma themselves, the then-Liberal immigration critic said, if those governments do not or cannot protect the Roma from attacks by organized groups of extreme right racist thugs, then Roma could legitimately claim refugee status.

This year, when Trudeau was the only leader to put the Harper government's cancellation of health benefits for refugees on the table in two of the campaign's leaders' debates, I, for one, was heartened. He had obviously retained the lessons he had learned when he held the opposition's immigration portfolio.

After Trudeau became leader, in 2012, I was puzzled at the Liberal's party's decision to market him as a kind of pure celebrity product, devoid of content. Back in January of 2015, I wrote a piece for rabble entitled: "Trudeau's Liberals Are about More Than Pure Celebrity." In it, I said that Trudeau:

> was well acquainted with the complex details of both immigration and refugee policy. Many MPs, and even more journalists, have a weak grasp of those issues. A great many are not even clear on the legal difference between immigrants and refugees. . . . As well, Trudeau spent a good deal of his time before entering politics working with

> environmental groups. That background does not show much in current Liberal policy. One suspects the party is spooked by the thrashing the Conservatives gave former leader Stéphane Dion over his "tax on everything." . . . But if Trudeau were in government one has the right to hope that a commitment to sound environmental policy and sustainable development would in some way inform Liberal policies.

The last time a Liberal government swept to power after nearly a decade of Conservative rule, in 1993, it too promised hope and change, anchored in a program of major infrastructure investments.

That Jean Chrétien-led government did deliver some of what it promised. But it also slashed the CBC and other federal institutions, radically reduced health and social transfers to the provinces, and completely ended longstanding federal support for some programs, such as public housing. Neither Chrétien nor any of his senior colleagues had ever mentioned they were planning to do any of that.

Let's hope the voters have better luck with the Liberal party this time.

Originally published on October 20, 2015.

2016 | Toronto Media Underestimating the Resilience and Strength of Black Lives Matter Leaders

Mark Brown

It was supposed to have been the tweet that stopped the earth from rotating. It was the tweet, twisted by mainstream media, that would make the city forget that on July 5, 2015, Andrew Loku, a forty-five-year-old father of five with a history of mental illness, was shot dead by Toronto police only minutes after they arrived on the scene.

We were supposed to have forgotten that on September 24, 2014, Jermaine Anthony Carby was shot and killed by a Peel Regional Police officer in Brampton, and neither of the officers involved will be charged with a crime. We were supposed to have overlooked names like Sophia Cook, Wade Lawson, Lester Donaldson, and others who received what many in the Black community would describe as an unjust and unnecessary level of violence via the barrel of a police officer's gun.

Finally, we should not have even been aware that Jean-Pierre Bony and Fredy Villanueva, both unarmed Black or brown men, were recently killed by the hands of police in Quebec. We were supposed to have turned our attention to the leaders of Black Lives Matter-Toronto (BLM-TO) and question their ability to lead as we fall in line. We were to believe that the leaders of BLM-TO, while under the immense pressure that comes with constructing societal change, are somehow not permitted to pray for restraint as they press forward.

"Why Are You Doing This Story?"

"Why are you doing this story?" asked Sandy Hudson, co-founder of Black Lives Matter Toronto, in an interview with veteran CP24 news reporter Jee-Yun Lee. Hudson was being interviewed about a tweet by co-founder Yusra Khogali in February of this year, in which Khogali wrote, "Plz Allah give me strength to not cuss/kill these men and white folks out here today. Plz plz plz."

Hudson went on to say that, for two weeks, people have been sleeping outside of the Toronto Police Headquarters under difficult circumstances, protesting deaths in our community, and that just the day prior, a Black man was killed by the hand of police in Montreal with not a single story from CP24. In addition, Hudson stated that Premier Kathleen Wynne has committed to reviewing the Special Investigations Unit (SIU), and mainstream media is focusing on a story put forth by a man who has made homophobic, Islamophobic, and misogynistic tweets in the past.

Hudson stated that he has effectively managed to manipulate media outlets to switch the story. She was referring to Jerry Agar, the Newstalk 1010 reporter, who discovered the tweet on Yusra Khogali's Twitter account and broke the story.

Despite repeated attempts, Lee could not get Hudson to switch the narrative from the police killings of Andrew Loku and Jermaine Anthony Carby. Even with the obvious frustration on Lee's face, she could not move Hudson from her original narrative of the disproportionate levels of police violence against the Black community.

Was Hudson supposed to break down under the pressure of the veteran reporter? Was she supposed to run away crying, taking with her the credibility of BLM-TO? I don't have an answer to those questions, but I am confident that, notwithstanding the young men on the executive of BLM-TO on this day, mainstream media clearly underestimated the strength of the Black women who lead the BLM-TO coalition.

A diamond in its earliest stages is under pressure as it is being formed in the earth. That pressure subsequently produces one of the strongest and most beautiful gems that the earth can provide. It has been said that similarly, the pressure and adversity experienced in the lives of Black women produce some of the strongest and most beautiful gems that the Black community has to offer. That gem was what was displayed by Hudson during the CP24 interview.

As a community, we can never forget how BLM-TO recently set up camp outside of the Metro Toronto Police Headquarters, protesting the SIU decision not to prosecute the officers involved in Andrew Loku's shooting or release their names. These sisters and brothers were beaten up by the police and dragged away from the barrels that safely housed the fires that kept them warm.

The police took both the barrels and their tents, and they were left to protest exposed to the cold. In response, BLM-TO acquired a sound system and a flatbed truck, organized a demonstration that brought hundreds if not thousands of people to the doorsteps of the police headquarters, and draped a banner stating "Black Lives Matter-Toronto" over the entrance to the flagship Metropolitan Toronto Police Headquarters.

In many ways, BLM-TO's resilience and strength are comparable to the resilience of those who experienced firsthand segregation and discrimination in the southern United States. The greater the opposition to the end goal, the stronger the resilience of BLM-TO becomes.

Whether they are blocking Toronto's Allen Expressway, camping out at the Toronto Police Headquarters or engaging in some other creative form of protest in order to get the message heard, history will not soon forget the sisters and brothers of BLM-TO who compelled a society to look at its own privilege and acknowledge that in addition to the other lives, all Black lives matter as well.

Originally published on April 14, 2016.

2017 | Tiny Houses, Enormous Statement

Erin Despard

Construction on the Kinder Morgan Trans Mountain Pipeline is due to start in BC any day, but another construction project is already underway along its path: members of the Secwepemc Nation and their supporters have begun building tiny houses. With one complete and a second underway, the Tiny House Warriors plan to build ten houses to assert their jurisdiction over the unceded lands the pipeline will traverse.

This is an ambitious but logistically feasible act of resistance, since the houses can be built in a short period of time, put on wheels, and transported to remote locations. It is also a beautiful one: tiny, off-grid homes symbolize a way of living that problematizes consumption and, in the rural locations for which these ones are destined, put domestic life in a relation to land which is strikingly modest. As the Tiny House Warriors put it, "land is home."

Despite their rural setting, these tiny houses reveal a surprising connection between Indigenous land claims and urban environmental politics. This connection resides in the contrast they establish between two very different ways of relating to land. In cities, where most land is transformed or concealed, we tend to see our surroundings in terms of property. This turns land into a volume of space or set of boundaries between which we are permitted to do what we please. So we seek out the largest houses or apartments we can afford and attempt to contain everything we need within them: not only spaces of shelter, repose, and food preparation, but also appliances and tools to enable domestic tasks, entertainment, communication and, increasingly, social contact. Our daily activities need not be connected to the land.

This makes it hard to see how the land contributes to our health and the quality of our lives, or how it *could* contribute to our sustenance, social relations, and opportunities for cultural expression. We mistake things like the quality of our groundwater, the air we breathe, the character of the soundscape, and the diversity of other beings who live among us for questions of a narrowly environmentalist concern, which are then susceptible to being opposed to other problems, such as unemployment or poverty. When land is not home, but something abstract or elsewhere, solutions to environmental problems are insurmountable because they seem to depend on an impossible co-ordination of individual actions—all of them inconvenient or expensive.

Worse, this relation to land prevents us from seeing how not only is a pipeline a future threat to the food and water sources of the Secwepemc people, it is an invasion and denigration of their home *before* anything goes wrong. The invisibility of urban land enables us to underestimate or disregard the extent of the injustices faced by First Nations communities across the country. It also makes it hard to see how concrete problems—such as water quality, poverty, and escalating suicide rates—arise out of and are sustained by government-enabled acts of dispossession. The Secwepemc houses remind us that these acts of dispossession—not just of land, but of the practices, social relations, and meanings it sustains—are not past but ongoing. And while it may be too late to give back much of what has been taken away, we don't have to keep taking; we can stop building pipelines or extracting resources where those activities are not welcome. If we did, we would be one very important step closer to rebuilding the conditions for equality and mutual respect between Indigenous and non-Indigenous Canadians. We might also find we have the impetus for inventing new ways of relating to land, even in the city.

In my urban neighbourhood, many people have small vegetable gardens. While home-grown food is more sustainable and meaningful than food bought at the grocery store, its production is constrained by the treatment of land as property. Not only is the yield small, but it is only available to people who have sunny yards or balconies. If, however, we saw land as something collectively held and valued, then we could cultivate not only gardens but also those spaces that contain, or *could* contain, fruit and nut-bearing trees, berries, mushrooms, and a myriad of edible weeds. If we did that, things like car exhaust, pollution from lawn chemicals, and laws against trespassing would become problems of immediate collective importance, regardless of the inconvenience or short-term costs of addressing them. We might also find that, in order to access and sustain urban food sources, we need to invent ways of communicating and sharing across social and cultural differences. Ways of working on the land, in other words, would become ways of working on ourselves.

Ultimately, tiny houses built in the path of an unwanted pipeline are a powerful symbol of resistance, but they also invite us to reflect on the fact that the destruction wrought by pipelines is due both to ways of living that perpetuate their apparent necessity and the fact that those ways of living help to conceal the extent of their impact. This makes us all responsible for putting an end to their construction, but it also suggests that in taking that on, we might at the same time begin to see a way forward with respect to certain apparently intractable urban problems. While land may never be home for city-dwellers in the way it is for the Tiny House Warriors, respecting that relationship is a step towards a more just and sustainable future for us all.

Originally published on October 11, 2017.

2018 | Valve-Turners Challenging Climate Crimes with Nonviolent Direct Action

Brent Patterson

On October 11, 2016, after months of studying how to undertake their action safely, five climate activists from Washington and Oregon shut down key pipelines used to transport tar sands oil from Alberta to the United States.

Their actions may have represented both frustration with and failure of the more common approaches of e-petitions, letters to the editor, and rallies. It could also be seen as a departure from some of the more symbolic forms of civil disobedience that rely primarily on people willingly waiting to be arrested and hoping for media coverage to spur further action.

The action wasn't focused on asking governments and corporations that are commonly deeply invested in these megaprojects to do the unlikely, but rather about community agency empowered by courage and a deep commitment to defending life and the planet.

As *The Nation* noted in an article on the action, "manually closing the emergency shut-off valves on tar sands pipelines in Washington, Montana, North Dakota, and Minnesota . . . surely stands among the boldest acts of nonviolent civil disobedience, on climate or any other issue, in memory." The activists stopped the pipelines from pumping as much as 15 percent of daily oil demand in the US, which calculates as roughly three million barrels of oil.

Three of the valve-turners—Ken Ward, Leonard Higgins, and Michael Foster—have now been tried and convicted of felony charges. Foster was sentenced to one year, but in the end, served six months in a state prison before being released on parole. The trial for the two remaining valve-turners—Annette Klapstein and Emily Johnston, along with support-team member Ben Joldersma—began on October 8.

Implications of the "Necessity Defence"

This trial could have historic significance, because while the previous three defendants were denied the "necessity defence," the court allowed Klapstein, Johnston, and Joldersma to argue that their actions were necessary and legally justified given the harm of climate change. The necessity defence acknowledges that while technically a crime was committed, it was done to prevent a greater harm.

The court's decision was also fascinating because the necessity defence requires proof that the accused was in imminent peril or danger, that there were no reasonable legal alternatives to the course of action undertaken, and that the harm inflicted by the accused was proportional to the harm avoided by the action.

While climate science arguably backs the imminent peril argument—official "legal" processes (including UN climate agreements) have failed to stop the planet heading towards a disastrous four degree Celsius global temperature increase—and turning a valve seems relatively minor in relation to the catastrophe of climate breakdown, the legal argument is a strictly limited one.

As such, a trial where defence of necessity arguments could have been fully argued created the anticipation of a precedent-setting moment that may have spurred further radical action in defence of the planet.

But rather than proceeding to trial and having witnesses called who could speak to climate crimes, the judge acquitted the three defendants. Still, the initial acceptance of the necessity defence could have implications for future antipipeline actions in both the US and Canada.

In May 2018, climate activist Tom Sandborn called on BC Supreme

Court Judge Kenneth Affleck to accept the "defence of necessity" argument after Sandborn was arrested and charged for blocking a gate at the Trans Mountain pipeline terminal in Burnaby. But Affleck said that the "excuse of necessity has no air of reality in these proceedings," its use must be "strictly controlled," a defendant must show there was "no other viable option" than the action, and there must be an "imminent risk of an immediate peril."

And despite the lack of free, prior, and informed consent highlighted in the United Nations Declaration on the Rights of Indigenous Peoples for the pipeline, and a DARA International study linking four hundred thousand deaths worldwide each year to climate change, the judge ruled, "The work is lawful and to call it a crime is just a slogan, not an argument."

Valve-Turning in Canada

There have been pipeline valve-turning actions in this country, too. These actions came out of the various protests against the Trans Mountain pipeline (as early as August 2011) and the Keystone XL pipeline (a symbolic civil disobedience action resulted in the arrest of 117 people on Parliament Hill in September 2011).

Despite these and other protests, those megaprojects moved ahead through regulatory processes. Climate science was pushed aside as billions of dollars of government subsidies to the fossil fuel industry continued, and mainstream media reinforced the notion of the tar sands as the economic driver of this country.

In December 2015, three men turned off a valve for the Enbridge Line 9 pipeline near St-Justine-de-Newton where it crosses the Ontario-Quebec border. They were charged with mischief, trespassing (breaking and entering), and obstruction. Then just two weeks later, three women turned a manual handwheel at a station in Sarnia and interrupted the flow of the pipeline for two hours.

In the latter case, Vanessa Gray, Sarah Scanlon, and Stone Stewart were charged with mischief endangering lives, a charge that carries a maximum penalty of life imprisonment, and mischief over $5,000. In January

2017, after a long court battle, the charges were withdrawn after Gray, Scanlon, and Stewart agreed to an eighteen-month court order to stay away from Enbridge property.

The now-defeated 1.1 million barrel-per-day Energy East pipeline would have been 4,500 kilometres in length, with a shut-off valve located every 30 kilometres along the route. That would have been about 150 shut-off valves susceptible to this type of action. The same would generally still hold true for the 300,000 barrel-per-day Line 9 pipeline that runs about 831 kilometres from Sarnia to Montreal and the Trudeau government's Trans Mountain pipeline that runs about 1,150 kilometres in length.

"Allowing [the necessity] defence will embolden other activists to commit crimes to further their causes," stated the Minnesota Chamber of Commerce about the court hearings for Klapstein, Johnston, and Joldersma.

Reflecting on the action, valve-turner Klapstein said: "What better thing to do with your retirement than attempt to salvage a habitable world for your children and grandchildren—I can't think of anything better."

Many others, young and older, may be thinking the same in this country.

As the world rapidly moves closer to the unstoppable, cascading impacts of climate breakdown and as governments continue to back the pipelines that fuel this devastation, there's a growing concern that the traditional methodologies and tactics of environmental NGOs are simply not commensurate to the task at hand.

That may spur a new grassroots direct action movement that will adopt a deeper systemic analysis and take bolder actions that involve greater risks of criminalization out of necessity and in proportion to the crisis.

Originally published on October 17, 2018.

2019 | The War on Women Is Still On

Antonia Zerbisias

On Wednesday, in the wake of the majority vote by twenty-five white Republican men in the senate of one of the most impoverished states in the US, #AlabamaAbortionBan was trending both south and north of the Canadian border.

Also trending, #Talabama.

That's because the Alabama abortion ban is one of the most draconian revocations of women's rights since women won the vote, a ban that would force even eleven-year-old victims of rape and incest to carry to term. These forced birthers want to take down *Roe v. Wade*, the 1973 US Supreme Court decision that rendered abortion bans unconstitutional. And why not try to reverse it now, what with Donald Trump and his Republican-controlled Senate packing the bench with conservative judges?

If successful, Alabama would bar "abortion and attempted abortion" by women "known" to be pregnant, whatever that means. The only exception is to "prevent a serious health risk to the unborn child's mother." As for doctors performing the procedure, they are looking at up to ninety-nine years in prison.

This latest vote follows other "heartbeat laws" in states across the South and Midwest. They essentially ban the procedure when a heartbeat is detected, usually about six weeks into a pregnancy, a period when many women do not yet even suspect that they are pregnant and aren't exactly rushing into clinics for ultrasounds. Indeed, so many states—Arkansas, Georgia, Ohio, Mississippi, North and South Dakota, Georgia, Kentucky and, now, Alabama and Missouri—have passed similar laws that the *New York Times* says abortion bans are now "mainstream."

Meanwhile, last week, the annual "March for Life" demonstrations, to which Catholic schoolchildren are bused in on the taxpayer dime, took place in Ottawa and in front of provincial legislatures across Canada. Catholic clergymen, MPs, and MPPs, including three provincial BC Liberals, spoke to the crowds.

But much was made of Ontario Conservative MPP Sam Oosterhoff's declaration at the Queen's Park protest that he would "fight to make abortion unthinkable in our lifetime." "To quote Dr. Seuss, 'A person's a person no matter how small,'" he waxed poetic—as if "Dr. Seuss" was a medical practitioner—when confronted by reporters later.

As for Ontario Premier Doug Ford, he just couldn't deal with the topic. He ducked NDP MPP France Gélinas during Question Period by tapping one of his ministers, who also dodged the question by talking about—what else?—the "job-killing, regressive carbon tax." Later, Ford's office issued a statement saying, "the government will not re-open the abortion debate."

Yet.

Meantime, in Alberta, Jason Kenney got the blessing of anti-choice groups in his successful run for the premier's post. Although he too has said he won't reopen the debate, recall that he was the founder of the "Pro-Life Caucus" on Parliament Hill. What's more, he appointed Adriana LaGrange, the former president of Red Deer Pro-Life, as his education minister.

So the war on women is still on, and my side is still losing.

We don't have equal pay. Lawmakers are trying to strip us of the right to control our bodies. And, when we do make babies, we have little access to safe and affordable child care. It's no wonder there are so many struggling single mothers and children who go hungry—in Canada, in 2019.

It's obvious: let women work and everybody profits, and that includes government coffers via taxation. It's been proven in Quebec. But in Ontario, Ford has cut child-care centres' general operating funding, which helps pay child-care workers, by $40 million. He has also slashed the capital funding portion, which is used to build new centres, by $93 million, leaving only $10 million in the kitty.

That's a full-frontal assault on women's rights, and a short-sighted one as well.

This week, Oxfam Canada urged federal parties to put publicly funded child care on the ballot. Citing a 2017 International Monetary Fund study, Oxfam reported that a 40 percent reduction in child-care costs would result in 150,000 highly educated stay-at-home mothers entering the workforce. This would increase Canada's GDP by two percentage points, or $8 billion a year.

But there's little chance this will happen, even in another "feminist" Justin Trudeau government. (Remember years and years of child-care promises by the federal Liberals in the 1990s?) But at least Trudeau openly stands firm on abortion rights. As for Conservative leader Andrew Scheer, there's no chance at all. In fact, given his "pro-life" beliefs, even abortion rights are at risk.

In Trumpland, legislative attempts to ban abortion are a blatant sign that women are under attack.

In Canada, the war on women is escalating, but slowly and stealthily, as Conservative governments form majorities across the country.

How soon before we see #Vaticanada trending on Twitter?

Originally published on May 17, 2019.

2020 | We Don't Need the Police. We Need Each Other

Reakash Walters and
Rachel Zellars

"Capitalism requires inequality, and racism enshrines it."
—Ruthie Gilmore

We are in an earth-shifting historical moment, unseen before in our modern world. On May 25, the world witnessed a Black man named George Floyd pinned against asphalt by three men in uniform, with Floyd calling out for his dead mother as he, knowingly, began to die. Collectively, a pandemic-isolated and hypervigilant world responded to his murder and a tsunami of other Black men and women murdered—while sleeping, jogging, or fleeing in terror—by those invested with the full force of the state.

Over the last two weeks, two cries for change have become standard refrains online and in the streets: "Defund the police!" and "Abolition now!"

The first is self-evident: It is a call to reduce police department annual budgets and redirect money to communities that, as Black Lives Matter co-founder Patrisse Cullors often says, have been "deeply divested from." In Canada, those communities are Black and Indigenous communities. Specifically, the call to defund is a demand for investment in social services for mental health, domestic violence, and homelessness—three areas where police officers are most often first responders and are crudely, violently insufficient, as the recent death of Regis Korchinski-Paquet confirms.

Abolition is a longer-term project in which prisons and police are permanently replaced with well-supported social services, community care networks, and mechanisms for accountability. The first is, of course, a precursor to the second, and while both refrains have become popular culture in our current moment, it is fair to say that, for many people, trepidation and sophomoric understandings underlie both ideas.

But what is it, really, that makes people so nervous about defunding the police and imagining a world without prisons?

The most concise answer is our commitment to individualism, a steely conditioning borne of the long arc of classical liberalism and, more recently, neoliberalism. This schooling renounces care and connection as the most essential needs of all human life. As radical as our protests and hubristic cries for abolition may be, most of us have no idea what to do when something harmful or violent occurs, including those of us who grew up with domestic violence.

We fear terrible things happening without a buffer. We fear violence without protection and a world where people who harm can continue to rage unchecked. Crucially, we have no idea what to do when harm occurs in our own homes. We lack the tools to navigate interpersonal violence. We run away from and sometimes discard friends, co-workers, and "bad" organizers on a whim. And we have even less of an idea what to do in order to shift or avert the very ground of violence—that is, to imagine and reshape material conditions that prevent, lessen, or obliterate violence itself.

In short, the fear that comes to us when we imagine a world without police is a fear of uncertainty that is tied to our own private spaces—our private relationships, private apartments, private homes, and insular communities, like the one in Portapique, Nova Scotia—that produce misogynists and mass killers. Our current moment is a clarion call for radical change and, equally, a reminder that "the revolution starts at home."

Transformative justice (TJ), the bedrock of abolition, is the learning model that guides us to begin reckoning with violence and harm, first, at the smallest scale and within all of our interpersonal relationships. At its most basic, TJ pushes us to find ways to respond to violence without generating more violence. It is not a script, because violence, while tied to identifiable conditions of scarcity and trauma, is emergent. TJ is a set of everyday practices that guide human relations to respond to harm and violence nonpunitively. It is a commitment to accountability rather than punishment. For many of our people who live with conditions of deep scarcity that are intractable, TJ is also harm reduction.

We can look to existing resources and stories for examples of what TJ looks like in real time. In the 2016 book *The Revolution Starts at Home,* Meiver De la Cruz and Carol Gomez share the story of a Korean immigrant named Sun-hi. Sun-hi was in an abusive marriage where she ended up losing her children and was at risk of deportation and homelessness.

Sun-hi reached out to her local network for care for support, and colleagues and activists built a long-term solidarity team around her. Their support strategy was grounded in knowledge of institutional racism, interpersonal racism, misogyny, and other forms of oppression. The actions they took to offer Sun-hi support over the next two years included support navigating the criminal legal system, translation services, physical protection from violence against her abusive husband, financial support, and socio-emotional support. Although Sun-hi ultimately lost custody of her children, she avoided deportation. Further, her twenty-seven-member team of support helped Sun-hi maintain her mental health, remain connected to her children, and develop personal advocacy skills.

In this way, TJ is about building and opting into communities of care right where we are, rather than replacing the police with a "more caring" institution. We must be willing to wander outside the nuclear family structure and take responsibility for the well-being and safety of those we call friends and even acquaintances. What would it mean to hold the intimacy and wellness of our friends as "our business" rather than allowing the domestic and interpersonal to remain the business of the state?

These are the very issues that elder organizers, such as Angela Davis and Joy James, have been centring in conversations and lectures regarding abolition over the last few years. During a luncheon in Halifax in the fall of 2018, Davis pointedly asked local prison abolition organizers, "How are you connecting it all, sexual violence and prison abolition?" While abolition is a political platform that invokes images of Black men in cages, our radical organizing histories teach us that such visioning is both partial and pathological.

Given the proliferation of popular and media representations of Black male criminality, as well as the radical growth of carceral institutions targeting Black men in the twentieth century, our communities often protectively encircled Black men in ways that forcefully undermined Black women's experiences with intraracial violence. Over time, the results were the relegation of gender violence to the private sphere and the castigation of individual histories as harmful distractions to community organizing.

Davis and James have reminded us that the outcomes of fighting for a world without police, without working in a parallel fashion to transform harm and violence at home, are communities that remain traumatized by both systemic and interpersonal violence. When we neglect to protect and prioritize Black women and children, we reinforce old hierarchies of organizing that gutted partnership violence from its agenda.

During a workshop on TJ in Montreal in March 2018, James offered a reflection on the role of gender violence in radical organizing that arose in the late 1960s:

> At this age, I am really grateful that younger people are now the leaders. Because I feel that you have the courage to call out contradiction where we would just endure decades of silence. This means that we just gave you a picture of the world that's not real because we buried the violence. And that's our complicity.

The work of reimagining and rebuilding safer communities is not simple or quick. We are standing on the shoulders of organizers from our past who brilliantly created free breakfast programs for our children but struggled to challenge the misogynist hierarchies that left Black women and children at risk.

In our current moment, opportunities for reflection and growth must be central to our abolitionist imaginings. Let us have the courage to dream, try, fail, try again, and fail better. As we demand the dismantling of our current policing systems, may we simultaneously cultivate robust communities of care. May we meditate on and take inspiration from the words of poet Gwendolyn Brooks: “We are each other’s harvest; we are each other’s business; we are each other’s magnitude and bond.”

Originally published on June 10, 2020.

Section 5: Activism and Indie Media: Pasts and Futures

Snapshots from rabble.ca's First Twenty Years

Kim Elliott and Matthew Adams

> "We kicked off rabble from the Quebec City demonstrations against the Free Trade Area of the Americas, so from the beginning we identified with social movements, something very new at the time."
>
> —Judy Rebick

On April 18, 2001, amid powerful street mobilizations against the third Summit of the Americas in Quebec City, a group of activists, journalists, and techies forged a groundbreaking way to do "news": 100 percent online, 100 percent open access, 100 percent committed to social change, and 100 percent from the ground up. From the beginning, rabble.ca chose not to participate in what its co-founders saw as the lie of media "neutrality." Instead, it would focus on stories of struggle, on stories about communities creating a more just world.

Those who launched rabble.ca were not the first to try to create a national left-wing newspaper. However, the exorbitant costs of printing, production, and distribution made it close to impossible for anyone to get much of anything off the ground. The emerging internet introduced new possibilities. By 2001, the Jean Chrétien Liberals had picked up on the Mulroney government's austerity agenda and were gutting Canada's social programs. Inequality was on the rise, and so was the concentration of media ownership. The national overtly right-wing media outlet, the *National Post*, had been launched in 1998. The New Politics Initiative would launch in the summer of 2001 to pressure the NDP to move to the left. Many had long felt it was time for a national progressive news media source.

There are many stories to tell in the history of rabble as an organization, and the question of how the site has been able to continue as an online publication for twenty years is a story in itself. Few pioneer organizations from the internet's early days still exist. Part of rabble's success had to do with the unique confluence of the political climate and emerging technologies. The site has been sustainable in part due to our approach to raising funds and establishing partnerships.

Without a doubt, we've also had our share of challenges: financial, political, and technological. We have had organizational changes, transitions, and burnouts. We've made mistakes along the way, and we are always learning. But our story is really about people—the thousands of people who have contributed to rabble as workers on the site, as journalists and producers, as interns, as advisors and volunteers, as donors and, most importantly, as readers, listeners, and viewers.

This book isn't a comprehensive history of rabble, and our chapter isn't either. We could fill these pages with just the names of people who have contributed to rabble as workers, board members, contributors, interns, advisors, and volunteers. Some of these people spent nearly two decades with the organization, others perhaps a few months on a journalism internship—all have been instrumental in rabble's history. Over the pages that follow, we briefly explore some of the trends, strategies, decisions, and challenges in building and sustaining one of the first—and predominantly women-led—independent online media sites in Canada.

From the beginning, one of the site's defining features has been active reader participation. Before Facebook, before Twitter, and certainly well before the first iPhone, rabble created "babble," a political virtual space for moderated discussion on the news of the day, built on the Ultimate Bulletin Board platform. Tens of thousands of people have opined, shared, posted, debated, and organized in babble.

Today, social media platforms have essentially replaced discussion boards. These corporate spaces are infamously "self-regulated," versus the approach we took at babble, where community moderators worked to keep discussions respectful and followed a commenting policy based on feminist, antiracist, queer-positive, anti-imperialist principles. Babble has remained a force throughout rabble's history and, for many years, has been a key place to take the pulse of Canada's political left.

From the beginning, rabble has been a bridge between social movements, the labour movement, and electoral politics: a space for debate and, we hope, learning about how those who are broadly considered "progressive" differ and where they may come together. This, by definition, means that rabble has constantly had to balance the expectations of readers from a variety of political and ideological left backgrounds. We often come under fire: Are we in the back pocket of the NDP? Do we exist to undermine the NDP? Are we too liberal? Are we too radical? Over the years, we have seen ourselves assumed to be many things. This is not unusual for journalism enterprises, but at times it has been a personal challenge for those who work in the organization—particularly for our editors. To be an editor of a publication like rabble requires not only journalism skills but also an understanding of Canada's social movements, an understanding of the power of journalism to support social justice, and a strong ethical commitment to fact-based reporting.

A consistent and significant challenge has been how to finance our online media venture. A one-time grant from the Atkinson Foundation gave rabble the funds to launch in 2001. Those funds ran out after the first year. Community support permitted the organization to continue, together with the relentless commitment of many of rabble's founding staff and volunteers to keep the organization going no matter what. We moved out of physical offices and became a virtual office by 2002. Staff faced difficult decisions: those who could do so took pay cuts, and many volunteered some of their time to keep the organization going. The real secret to rabble's longevity has been a small team of passionate part-time staff, working with a very engaged volunteer board, activists, and donors from across the country. It is what Judy Rebick once called the "magic" of rabble's success.

The website has always been free to read, watch, and listen to. Our philosophy is that movement news should not be hidden behind a paywall. In 2004, rabble registered federally as a nonprofit organization, having moved on from our original organizational host, the Canadian Centre for Policy Alternatives, two years earlier. We began to push for membership support, and our crowdfunding has been critical for rabble's ability to sustain itself. To keep our content accessible to all, we ask for donations from those who can afford to give.

As nonprofit progressive online media, traditional sources of revenue that many media outlets in Canada have relied on were not available: grants for digital publications are a fairly recent phenomenon. We are not a project of a wealthy founder or foundation. When advertising looked like a small but potentially sustainable source of funding, rabble could not accept just any advertiser—a large buy from American Apparel, for example, led to a campaign on babble exposing working conditions in the company at the time. Media engaged in exposing the injustices of capitalism and dedicated to seeking solutions to inequality will not ultimately find support in advertising or angel investors.

The labour movement has been a critical financial contributor to Canada's social movements, and they have been important supporters over the years. Most of rabble's "sustaining partners"—a recognition program developed by rabble's long-time president, Duncan Cameron—are unions. Because we understand the critical importance of transparency as progressive media, rabble has always listed its major community funders in annual reports and on the website itself. The vision of organizations like the Anarres Workers' Co-op and individuals like Wayne MacPhail has allowed for much experimentation with new media, despite our small budget and team, and is what has permitted rabble to grow, evolve, and experiment with new forms of journalism over the years.

In the early years, it wasn't yet clear how multimedia would dominate the internet, but rabble remained determined to expand the ways that people got and shared the news. Our first decade was a period marked by rapid technological change and innovation, as the possibilities of the internet grew. For our part, limited financial resources opened our eyes to innovation as a way to survive and thrive. In 2005—the year that Apple added podcasts to iTunes—we formed the rabble podcast network (rpn). The rpn launched with about twenty podcasts. Shows included the very popular "needs no introduction"—recordings of talks and lectures from the progressive community—and "the ruckus," our own musical show that garnered tens of thousands of downloads (a big number back then!), and "rabble radio." The rpn concept was developed by MacPhail, who was also instrumental in a great number of other tech innovations at rabble, including a book club in the virtual reality space of Second Life, rabbletv, and the award-winning e-book versions of our annual "Best of rabble" books.

The rabble Book Lounge was created in 2005 by editor Lisa Rundle, with the slogan "bound but not gagged." The original iteration of the Book Lounge included a combination online book and "baubles" store (in partnership with a nonprofit worker co-op, the Catalyst Centre, and York University Bookstore). The store, like much early e-commerce, didn't last. Like many booksellers, it could not compete with the likes of Amazon. The Book Lounge continues to highlight the work of Canadian indie publishers through book reviews, interviews, and podcasts.

The mid-aughts was a particularly challenging time for media in Canada. Media ownership concentration had reached its apex by 2005. In 2006, the Senate Committee on Canadian media released its final report, warning about

> the potential of media ownership concentration to limit news diversity and reduce news quality . . . diminishing employment standards for journalists (including decreased job security, less journalistic freedom, and new contractual threats to intellectual property); and difficulties with the federal government's support for print media and the absence of funding for the internet-based news media.

Traditional media was becoming more conservative as it became more concentrated. Shortly after our launch, 9/11 happened and brought with it a crackdown on activists around the world. Neoconservative ideology grew a new foothold in the country by 2006, with the election of Stephen Harper's first minority government. The probusiness, proconservative bias of the media grew more pronounced. The *Globe and Mail* and other major media editorials supported Harper's reelection time after time.

Amid these changes in corporate media, rabble continued to focus on activism and social movements. In 2008, we hosted a "media democracy" event in Toronto, where hundreds of activists participated in a full day of workshops in collaboration with community organizations, culminating in a live concert and celebrating the launch of a newly redesigned website: rabble 2.0, which moved us to the open-sourced Drupal platform.

Online independent media was growing around the world. Some in Canada—Straight Goods news and the newly formed Toronto Media Co-op—identified as unapologetically left. Other new online media sought to define their place amid mainstream media and resisted the progressive moniker for a time. All of these outlets were small, operating on, in rabble's case, less than the salary of a single public television news anchor.

For us, it was also a time of organizational transition. Judy Rebick had retired as volunteer publisher by the end of 2005, and she was open about having experienced burnout from running an independent online media site. Facing a second financial crisis and discussion of whether we should close our doors, a new generation of part-time staff ran the day-to-day operations, including the two of us. We forged an alliance with the progressive Media Consortium (TMC)—the largely foundation-funded US progressive media organization that included Alternet, Mother Jones, and Bitch Magazine.

Our relationship with TMC offered us a network to explore new media models during the whirlwind of tech developments that would characterize the early to mid-aughts and a media community with which to share our experiences. We had already seen how Facebook initially brought us new readers, and we joined Twitter shortly after it launched. Online video was emerging at this time too, and we agreed to become an early account holder on the start-up Mogulus (later to become Livestream.com), whose founder we met at a TMC meeting. The decision was typical of rabble's mode of operating: creativity made up for lack of cash flow, and rabble benefited from a grandparented account on Livestream.com for many years. The same innovation found rabble being one of the first to launch a news app (which is no longer active) in partnership with Spreed Inc., which was featured in MacWorld Magazine.

On the anniversary of the invasion of Iraq in 2008, rabbletv launched to cover the World Against War antiwar protests. The launch became a key part of Canadian participation in the antiwar movement. rabbletv offered live streaming of Canadian antiwar rallies. We were right there—on the street—searching for wireless signals with bulky equipment to interview people.

A few months later, when the Conservative government banned British MP George Galloway from entering Canada as part of his antiwar speaking tour, rabble used our Mogulus account to get around the ban. Galloway spoke from Democracy Now!'s New York studio to the scheduled event venues across Canada on rabble's channel. It was a ground-breaking moment that revealed the grassroots potential of the new technology, and it made national television news in Canada. From these events, rabble grew a partnership with the start-up that produced Flip video cameras that—in a time before smartphones were widely available—allowed us to build multimedia teams to cover activist events. In an article for the organization's tenth anniversary, journalist and former intern Mai Nguyen explained: "rabbletv was truly a breakthrough for rabble, independent media and the anti-war movement in Canada."

The advent of smartphones brought even more opportunities to experiment with multimedia coverage. The 2010 Winter Olympics in Vancouver were highly contested by social justice, antipoverty, environmental, and Indigenous rights groups, and rabble's team was on the ground with video, podcasts, photos, live-tweeting, and reporting. We hosted and live-streamed to activists across the country the heated discussions about strategy and tactics.

Our coverage of the Olympics proved to be a training ground for our street coverage of the G20 Summit, held in Toronto later that summer. More than ten thousand activists gathered on June 26, 2010, to protest globalization. We live-streamed the Council of Canadians' "Shout Out for Global Justice" event held at Massey Hall in partnership with Democracy Now! Tens of thousands of people around the world watched the stream. Canadian law enforcement responded to the anti-G20 activism with what would become the largest mass arrest in Canadian history. Arrestees faced human rights violations as they were detained in temporary holding facilities. Staff and freelancers from rabble followed the protests—blogging from the streets, capturing and sharing images, video, podcasting "nearly live" interviews with newly released detainees, and live-tweeting the events as they unfolded.

We continued to cover the aftermath in the years that followed, using tools like "Cover it Live" to provide immediate reports from the G20 court challenge. Our news editor at the time, Cathryn Atkinson, co-ordinated over twenty writers, bloggers, and photographers, both inside the summit itself and on the streets of Toronto. Having covered rallies and riots as a journalist in Britain, she understood what was happening from her base in BC:

> rabble operates as a virtual office so I was thousands of kilometres away. From the beginning to the end I watched the situation deteriorate online, and having been in similar situations I could easily imagine what was going to happen, though I was surprised and appalled by how badly the police behaved. . . . Because of that my first concern was for the safety of the reporters we'd sent out and for the stories that came in. It was a flood of information the entire weekend, and we tried to coordinate it and assess what was going on. One of our reporters was taken aside by police but released, and luckily no one was arrested or hurt in the end. It's surprising, given how many others were injured and arrested.

Social movements were producing incredible tools and building their own websites to share them. In 2010, with the support of the Douglas Coldwell Foundation, we launched an open-source, wiki-based collection of "how to" guides, workshop outlines, and other tools to help build movement infrastructure. This collection of activist tools grew when the United Steelworkers union supported its expansion into what would become the "Lynn Williams Activist Toolkit," named after one of the most influential North American union leaders of the twentieth century.

The Toolkit remains active today with a renewed focus on amplifying the work of Canadian social movements.

On our tenth anniversary in 2011, frustrated with mainstream media's continued support of Stephen Harper, we believed Canadians urgently needed a reporter on Parliament Hill who would cover "news for the rest of us." With financial support from our readers, the Canadian Auto Workers, and the Canadian Union of Public Employees, rabble sent award-winning journalist Karl Nerenberg to cover federal politics on Parliament Hill. Karl posted over eighty stories in his first year with his column "Hill Dispatches." With Karl covering federal politics, our coverage expanded.

While most Canadian news outlets have maintained their business sections, most have abandoned their labour beat. In contrast, rabble has long included a labour section reporting on workers' issues from workers' perspectives, and in 2012 we launched a labour reporting internship. This paid internship, sponsored by the labour union Unifor, offered an important learning opportunity and provided a solid base for coverage of emerging labour issues in Canada.

As we moved into our second decade, new forms of social movements emerged that drew on new technologies and social media. Internally, we began to experience the challenge of aging website infrastructure, of managing an immense content archive (including taking on Straight Goods' content archive when they shut down in 2013), and further organizational transformation with a new generation of workers.

When protests erupted across North Africa and the Middle East beginning in December 2010, the movement that became known as the Arab Spring opened the world—and our contributors—to social media's potential to enact social change. When Occupy Wall Street emerged in 2011, rabble was there—we dedicated a special section of the site to coverage of the movement. When students in Quebec launched massive organized resistance against tuition hikes in 2012—the Maple Spring—rabble featured extensive coverage, including on-the-ground reporting. When Idle No More began in November 2012, rabble devoted its coverage to the actions happening across Turtle Island, from Chief Theresa Spence's first hunger strike in Ottawa to food security actions in the North and the RCMP raid of a peaceful blockade in Elsipogtog. In 2015, we would partner with Toronto's Aboriginal Legal Services to launch a series called "Reconciliation Resolution," which built on the release of recommendations by the Truth and Reconciliation Commission on Indian Residential Schools.

Climate change movements had also grown in size and diversity during these years. International climate summits helped grow youth leaders that understood the racial and economic implications of climate justice. In Canada, Indigenous-led climate justice activism took on an increasing leadership. Healing Walks were held in the Northern Alberta tar sands to bring together solidarity among Indigenous communities and allies. We covered these events with new "issue" pages on the site, bringing original contributors and reprinting some of the best coverage from elsewhere.

Following on the mass movements of Occupy and Idle No More, rabble continued to report on emerging social movements, from Black Lives Matter to the #MeToo movement. One of the ways we responded to these movements was by creating the Jack Layton Journalism for Change Fellowship for emerging writers in partnership with the Institute for Change Leaders.

Canadian news media continued to face challenges, as occasional layoffs and buyouts of smaller outlets morphed into mass layoffs and widespread newsroom closures. The online media world was not immune to these financial challenges, and many media start-ups came and went.

The Harper era ended as the Justin Trudeau Liberals came to power on a platform that pulled on major progressive issues that had won the NDP Official Opposition status in 2011. Social movements had come together as never before to defeat the Harper government. We live-streamed the launch of the Leap Manifesto, a multisectoral movement to pressure political parties to support a climate justice agenda in the lead-up to the 2015 election. We co-hosted and provided live-streaming of debates and found over a million readers visiting the site during and after that year's federal campaign.

As these new social movements evolved, so did right-wing extremism and Islamophobia, the latter growing over decades but fuelled anew by the 2016 election in the US. On January 29, 2017, the attack on the Islamic Cultural Centre of Quebec City seemed the culmination of the rise of Islamophobia that had become political fodder for the right. As Ehab Lotayef wrote in rabble at the time, "More, or most, of the blame falls on the media and the politicians who are followed by thousands, and sometimes millions, and who use their popularity and following to fuel the flames of fear, hatred and anger to make political gains or to further their career."

Right-wing activists had been experimenting with new kinds of media in Canada. Sun News launched on the day of rabble's tenth anniversary. By 2015, it had closed, and right-wing commentator Ezra Levant launched *Rebel News* just in time for that year's federal election. The emerging niche of ideologically-based websites on the right would replace former blogs and would contribute to what has become the crisis of "fake news," a growth that has without a doubt been supported by the anti-elite, anti-science conservatism that Canada experienced during the Harper conservative years.

From its inception, rabble's relationship to our readers has been different from that of most media. Our founding mission "to grasp the real power of the internet: people" has put readers in a unique place of ownership. Over the years, the business model and the way we answer to the community—whether babble or bloggers—has created a special set of challenges. Rabble answers to its audience in a way that few other media do.

We have felt the full force of our readers' views on many occasions. One of the earliest examples was the babble strike of 2004. Discussion board participants made their voices heard in reaction to a staffing decision, and babblers went on "strike." The action resulted in a new discussion board, which later split into a third discussion board. It was perhaps the first online "strike" on a discussion board—and a lesson about the currency that engaged individuals hold online.

We have also grappled with what it means to provide a broad space for progressive views. Who blogs is often a question of privilege. When we opened our blogging and podcasting platforms as self-publishing networks—following the community media model in this way—we established contracts that outlined respect for our journalism policy. But we did not foresee the challenges we would face offering unmediated platforms to writers and communities with opposing views. A case in point was a situation in Ukraine. In 2014, as people took to the streets in Ukraine, rabble's bloggers took different stances. The Canadian left was divided, and rabble found itself facing a boycott for carrying two antithetical left views. The Ukraine boycott did not get much public notice, but it took enormous resources to resolve.

We learned the hard way that self-published content compromised our editors' agency and made it difficult to maintain the quality and journalistic integrity of published content. Arguments between bloggers occupied too much editorial time and demoralized editors and staff. In the case of writings about sex work, we found ourselves in a situation that escalated rapidly. We were hit with two opposing boycotts—one calling for a writer's dismissal based on anti–sex work and transphobic views she expressed, and a second defending the writer on the basis of "free speech." Both boycotts and the ensuing discussion of them played out on social media and our babble forum. Ultimately, the writer violated our journalistic policy, and that put an end to the relationship. It was a particularly divisive period. We recognize the hurt and anger caused by having published this writer on rabble and that we damaged relationships with communities that we value. As a result of these experiences, we no longer carry self-published blogs.

The era of self-published blogs was already coming to an end. Even the *Huffington Post*, an outlet built on blogs, ceased carrying them in 2018. As their editor commented, "Open platforms that once seemed radically democratizing now threaten, with the tsunami of false information we all face daily, to undermine democracy."

We are under no illusions about the increasingly challenging times we live in. But we also have optimism and hope for strong movement alliances, as new generations discover the necessity of critical thinking and solidarity.

As we move into the uncharted, evolving territory of the pandemic and post-pandemic world, we are at a turning point on racial and economic inequality, climate justice, and perhaps a new green economy. We meet rabble's twentieth anniversary with the determination to strengthen, nurture, and learn. Supporting the next generations of Canada's reporters has always been core to rabble's mandate, and that will continue.

We look back, with much pride, on twenty years of covering the news progressively and creatively, using every new technology available, and breaking new boundaries. Our launch at the Quebec Summit of the Americas in 2001 gave rabble a special focus and mission that continues today: to amplify the voices of resistance struggles and movement-focused news.

"More Power Than We Were Made to Believe": A Conversation with Judy Rebick, Leah Gazan, and Eriel Tchekwie Deranger

The most successful social movements harness a range of tactics: leveraging people power and organizing in the streets, shifting public discourse through the media, and, sometimes, electing insurgent politicians to formal political leadership. In the spring of 2020, we sat down with three activists working towards system change in these realms: rabble co-founder Judy Rebick, NDP Member of Parliament Leah Gazan, and executive director of Indigenous Climate Action Eriel Tchekwie Deranger. The five of us met over video conference to reflect on the future of movement organizing and the power of independent media.

TURNER: Judy, you were part of the group that launched rabble in 2001. The site's co-founders were both long-time activists and professional mediamakers. Can you tell us about your relationship to activist journalism?

REBICK: The start of my activism was the *McGill Daily* in the 1960s. As a child, writing was always an outlet for me, and as a young woman, I spent a lot of time fighting against restrictions on me as a female. So the beginning of my activism was student journalism. Later I dropped the idea of journalism because I was too radical for the mainstream media.

But after thirty years of activism, I decided to try it again and took a job as the left-wing host of a debate show on the CBC. At the end of my time at the CBC in 2000, I was part of a group of people who were trying to organize an independent national newspaper—we were thinking of creating a weekly national newspaper for the left, because it was very hard to get left-wing voices in the mainstream media. But a national paper was going to cost way more than the funding we had. I thought maybe the internet would be a good medium for a left-wing newspaper. At the time, Facebook and Twitter didn't exist. I organized meetings with alternative media people in every city I went to and always made sure half of the people in the room were under thirty—because younger people understood the internet better than the rest of us. They all said the same thing: "If it's not interactive, we're not interested."

For us to have an interactive site, we had to have a moderator who could post comments. So we set it up and decided we should launch rabble with stories from the ground in Quebec City because there was a massive antiglobalization demonstration, the biggest one since the Battle of Seattle two years prior. Because we were the only left-wing media that was on the ground, we got a lot of attention.

TURNER: Leah and Eriel, which moments in your lives have shaped your experiences as activists?

GAZAN: My father was a Holocaust survivor from Holland, one of five surviving children after the war. My mother was a Chinese Lakota woman from Wood Mountain Lakota First Nation who, at age five, ended up on the streets. I grew up in the movement. I don't remember a time in my life where I wasn't participating in actions, whether it was the anti-apartheid movement or when I was eighteen years old, camping out on the legislative grounds during the Oka crisis in solidarity. It's just who I am. Being born an Indigenous person in Canada is a political act; you're born into the struggle. The struggle is not something I became interested in, It's something that I feel like I haven't had a choice but to do.

So I've spent my life fighting for the human rights of all peoples. I'm almost fifty years old, I'm not young anymore, and all my life I've been fighting. I grew up with parents who fought their whole life until they died. Then, about five years ago, I thought, "why am I doing this?" And I thought, all right, I'm fighting for the right to joy. I'm fighting for the right to joy for myself, for my kids, for our community, for people, for people I don't know. Lately, I've been trying to reframe my actions around measures of joy instead of measures of suffering.

DERANGER: When people are deemed activists, it's usually not a title that they were striving for. It's something we've found ourselves in. One of the comments that resonates with me the most is what Leah said about being born Indigenous into this world: you're born into a community of resistance. I am no stranger to that. My family, like many Indigenous families, was one that struggled a lot. My dad is a residential school survivor, and he was also placed in an experimental tuberculosis hospital for four years as a child. He went to residential school right after he got out of the hospital, but he wound up being one of the lucky ones because he ran away from the residential school and hid in the bush with his dad. My dad's resistance to systems of oppression started at eight years old, as a very small child. My father and mother met through the American Indian Movement. They were both active within that movement, and in the 1960s and 1970s and they moved to Canada to occupy my family's traditional trap line, which was in the pathway of uranium exploration and development in Northern Saskatchewan. They occupied those lands for six years.

My entire upbringing was protests, rallies, occupations, just like Leah describes. I was at the occupations on the legislature grounds during the Oka crisis and my family actually harboured refugees. But the first time I took an act of personal resistance, I was seven years old. I was in school, and we were supposed to do a book report. I was looking through the books in the library and I pulled out a book full of Native stereotypes. I didn't say anything to my teacher, but I brought the book home and in my report, I wrote about how the book had stereotypes in it and that Native people don't live in teepees and use smoke signals, that we're just like everyone else and that the book was racist. It resulted in the school calling my mom, the book being pulled from the school library, and my mom being called in to do cultural sensitivity training for the students. This early act of personal resistance led me to believe that I have power as an Indigenous woman and that my voice, when I speak up, actually has an impact.

At twenty-two years old, I had a meeting with some members of parliament in Ottawa as a part of an Aboriginal youth delegation. The MPs were talking about how they were trying to get more Indigenous people into politics and they kept asking, "What are your thoughts? How do you feel about that? Was it working?" I just said to them, "You know what would be really good? If Canada didn't just have political parties that tried to amalgamate Indigenous voices. But if we were given actual voices within parliament with our own seats and our own parties run by our own people."

For me, activism is in my blood, but it's in my blood not because I'm altruistic or righteous, it comes from places of trauma. It comes from resiliency, from surviving oppression. But it also comes from seeing light on the other side and seeing the power that we hold, and from looking for ways to create platforms to amplify the power that comes from our communities.

REUSS: Judy, what's your perspective on the impacts of the social movements we've seen rise up in the last twenty years?

REBICK: rabble started at the height of the antiglobalization movement. That movement—against corporate globalization—was strong and growing. There was nowhere that meetings with world political leaders and financiers—the G8, the World Trade Organization—could happen where there weren't huge protests. But six months after rabble was founded came the September 11 terrorist attacks. And September 11 shifted everything. The antiglobalization movement declined. All of a sudden, any activist was a terrorist, and we saw the rise of Islamophobia. Rabble was founded at a moment when social movements were powerful, and it was difficult because there was a precipitous decline in movement organizing some years after September 11. What did happen in that period of time was the explosion of social media, of the internet.

The big social movement that emerged next was Idle No More, which was the first movement that was fuelled in a big way by the power of the internet. Idle No More became a hashtag, and the movement spread in a way that we hadn't seen happen for a long time. We started to see movements that were organized in physical space turn into movements that started to be organized online. Black Lives Matter was also organized online. This is not to say that these movements didn't have demonstrations, but that we saw a big changes in the way movements were organized, and as a result, who could be involved in movement organizing.

The antiglobalization movement, for example, was organized by mostly young people and with support from the unions. And if you'll remember, there was a big division between the labour movement and youth. In Quebec City in 2001, we saw a terrible thing happen: the labour movement was holding press conferences and denouncing the anarchists in the street, even though the people in the streets weren't just anarchists, but thousands and thousands of young people who were becoming radicalized. Those of us in the streets had to defend ourselves against three days of attacks by the police, who were using tear gas and beating people. And yet the labour movement didn't support us, and we had these heated debates about diversity of tactics.

Then came Idle No More and Black Lives Matter, which, in some ways, represented a new form of online organizing. Now we're seeing something quite different, I think. I think what's going to emerge out of 2020 is going to be a global, anticapitalist, antiracist, feminist movement. That's what I hope, anyway.

DERANGER: It's really interesting to watch how as social movements have started to build momentum and shift the Overton window, the range of policies and ideas that are politically acceptable in the mainstream, we have also seen the rise of fascist, oppressive policies and political leadership. These politicians and policies represent an attempt to maintain the systems that built the countries that we're in, systems of colonialism, capitalism, and patriarchy. In the environmental movement, we've seen this really happen over the last five years. The labour movement, the movement for Indigenous rights, and environmentalists have started to come together, to build relationships with progressive leaders in government. And we're starting to see shifts happen. The fact that we even got a bill tabled on the United Nations Declaration on the Rights of Indigenous Peoples (UNDRIP), Bill C-262, pays homage to that movement work. The fact that we're seeing Indigenous communities have our rights recognized in multiple different ways is evidence of strong social movements. But while Indigenous rights have been recognized, they have not been implemented, and those are two different things. We have a lot written on paper, but it's the implementation, the follow-up, that's the most important. And as we've made that progress, we've also seen the rise of fascism. In Alberta, the ushering in of the United Conservative Party (UCP) government in 2019 has taken us ten steps backwards from the slow progress that we made over the last ten to fifteen years.

Independent media has become such a game changer in the way that we fight back. It enables us to fight back, to have conversations. During the coronavirus pandemic, as we socially distance, independent media allowed us to respond to the oppressive measures that conservative and neoliberal politicians tried to slip through the cracks in a time of crisis.

But that isn't to say that fascists and the right wing aren't trying equally as hard. Just because we have strength in numbers and are starting to build these collective, coalesced movements doesn't mean we've won. We have to keep pushing harder and further to actually create systemic change that goes beyond writing the policy on paper and work towards implementation of what needs to come next. What are the next steps that need to happen so that we don't elect more conservative, fascist political leadership in this country? What are we going to do once we've won the space? That's what excites me about the future. That's where independent media spaces that elevate those voices, the voice that I found at seven years old, is critical.

People talk about climate change, about environmental destruction, and about human rights as if these are all different things. But they're all propagated through systems of colonization and entrenched white supremacy predicated on hyperindividuality and the accumulation of wealth, notoriety, and fame. These systems drive capitalism and patriarchy. And we have to fight these systems, because they are driving the climate crisis, which is causing harm to Indigenous populations and the planet as a whole.

Ultimately, I think that we are winning. Right now, we're in a moment where the coronavirus pandemic has caused us to be like "Oh, balanced budgets, what's that?" This pandemic is forcing us as a whole, as society, as a species, to reevaluate what is important and how we move and react to these systems of economic crashes. I'm really excited by the opportunities, but also terrified by what the future brings.

GAZAN: For the last few years, I actually was one of the key lobbyists for Bill C-262, the legislation that sought to see the full adoption and implementation of the UNDRIP. When I was lobbying for Bill C-262, I just felt so hopeful for the first time in my life. People from all walks of life, all different cultural backgrounds, colours, ethnicities, came together to fight for this bill for which we were long overdue. And I think a big part of that was the fact that alternative media outlets really led the charge in terms of communicating and informing others about UNDRIP.

Right now, with the pandemic, I think we have an opportunity to change things so that we never go back to the way things were. Policies like a universal income for all people, for example. These ideas come about not because of elected officials, but because of people in movements. And right now, I see a movement and a unity of people coming together over social media and alternative media platforms to highlight issues that are often ignored by mainstream media outlets.

I sit in the House of Commons and I hear my minimum human rights up for debate almost on a daily basis. The House of Commons is one of the most racist, oppressive environments I've ever been in. Indigenous rights are recognized in the Canadian constitution, but they are not respected. In this country, it's been normalized to question the human rights of people, whether it be Palestinians or Indigenous peoples. We've got a long way to go and I think alternative media is saving the day. Progressive media outlets are critical right now in terms of storytelling. Alternative media provides a different side of the story and forces people to think in a different way, to question systems that continue to marginalize and oppress people, in real time. Take the Wet'suwet'en solidarity protests, for example. If it wasn't for alternative media outlets like Ricochet, for example, most people would not have known about how the RCMP were dismantling the encampments and restricting movement on Wet'suwet'en territory.

TURNER: Has the mainstream media gotten any better at covering stories than they used to be? And if so, in what way?

GAZAN: I think that the mainstream media has morphed in many ways. Many mainstream outlets now have Indigenous hubs, for example. But I think it's been the rise of alternative media that has allowed us to tell stories that never have been told before and allowed perspectives to be presented that have been left out of mainstream media in a dangerous way. I'll give you a current example: Eishia Hudson, a sixteen-year-old young girl in Winnipeg was shot by police in April of this year. She had robbed a liquor store with some other young people and stolen a vehicle, but she ended up being killed by police. And if it hadn't been for social media and alternative media sources, this story of police violence would not have been told. These stories of police violence are often not told from an unbiased perspective in the mainstream media. If we want to really tell these stories, we have to amplify all sides and voices.

In Canada right now, during the pandemic, if it wasn't for the work of alternative media, we wouldn't see enough criticism of our government's response to the crisis. As an example, the Liberals allocated $305 million for Indigenous communities. That sounds like a lot of money, but it was less than one percent of the $82 billion coronavirus relief package. And this fact has not been scrutinized enough in mainstream media. We often see a political bias in a lot of the mainstream media that has traditionally served the right wing.

REBICK: I have a different take from Leah. When rabble started, I was on television: I had a voice in the mainstream media and I was openly radical. I didn't try to fit in. I don't think somebody like me would be in the mainstream media now. If you look at the CBC, for example, the range of opinion is small. We went through a period of time where there were no left, radical voices in the mainstream, and we're still kind of there. I do think the media has been paying a lot more attention to social movements than they used to. For example, youth climate organizing has been quite well covered in the mainstream media, fact-wise. But where I think the mainstream media derives its power now is more in interpreting what's happening, not just reporting on it.

Right now, I think there's real discussion and debate going on about what happens after the pandemic and how we deal with this crisis. The left has actually had more influence in the last two weeks in Canada than I've seen in my whole life. The Canada Emergency Response Benefit (CERB), for example, comes out of the Canadian Centre for Policy Alternatives and the unions. It's not coming from the Liberal Party. It's not coming from the corporations. While we would like the see the CERB cover more people, especially poor people, it is nevertheless the closest program we have ever had to a Guaranteed Annual Income. These ideas that the government has been pressured to use to support people come out of the left. I think we're in a strong position—as long as we're aware of what's coming, which is disaster capitalism. There's going to be huge pressure for austerity, and we have to be ready. And now, of course there is a massive movement against anti-Black racism and against police violence, so there is a lot of pressure on the media to be more representative. This will mean more Black journalists, I hope.

In a way, alternative media can help us to discuss and figure out what we should be demanding right now. Should we be demanding an annual guaranteed income? There are people on the left that don't agree with that idea. That's a big debate we need to have. We are having it now in alternative media. There will always be other big debates that need to happen. The important role that independent and alternative media play is to give us a place to discuss and to develop these ideas.

REUSS: I was recently talking to a tenant activist about organizing for protections during the pandemic, and she said that it felt like almost overnight, everything was put on the table in terms of what is possible. In some senses, the left is in a position to fight for policies and change that we didn't think we could successfully win even just two weeks ago. With that in mind, what do you want to see us win tomorrow, and how do we get there?

DERANGER: As Judy said, we're in this moment where all these things are happening—and the fact that social movements are actually able to see victory on the horizon right now has revealed that all of these things that we were told were impossible and immovable, are actually possible and moveable. We're also at a challenging point where people are realizing that the systems that our economy relies on, that we rely on for the health and safety of our communities, are fallible. These systems are completely fractured, and they do very little for the long-term security of our communities. They do little to uphold our rights, whether we're Indigenous, people of colour, marginalized, or communities living in poverty. These systems don't serve our interests anymore.

And yet, we are the ones holding up the very structures that people who have power and money rely on. Who are the essential workers in this crisis? It's janitorial workers, it's food service workers. It's grocery store workers. It's the people who are packing our packages and delivering them to our homes. It's the nurses, the doctors, and the educators who are scrambling for ways to continue educating our children. And yet, these are some of the most oppressed workers, who have some of the weakest rights and some of the lowest wages. We really have to reimagine what these systems and structures that make society function look like, so that we don't have to come back to the very systems and the very structures that have oppressed us to support us in a moment of crisis.

When we can release ourselves from the empire that has oppressed us, then we are imagining a future that is just. When we are not voices on the internet, but when we have power behind those voices. When we are not only saying what we want but asserting it and putting it into action. When communities say "no" to a project, and the project doesn't go through. And when communities say they want a project, that project is supported and delivered. When we stabilize local economies so that communities have sovereignty over energy, food security, and housing.

The pandemic has shown that our current economic and political structures do very little to support community sovereignty. It has also shown that we have a ton more power than we were made to believe. If we don't realize this moment as a moment of opportunity, a moment to take power and leverage it to move towards a just future, not just for our communities, but for the planet, then we are squandering a major opportunity.

GAZAN: As Eriel says, people are awakening to the growing corporate dictatorship that we live in. One only has to look at the fact that this current prime minister has given billions of dollars to the fossil fuel industry at the beginning of a public health crisis. Yet, as an MP, I have to beg to try and get services to ensure women and kids are safe in my community in Winnipeg. I think we have everything on the line right now. I will measure our accomplishments through action. I think we need to speak truth to power. We need to name the systems we need to undo. And we have to fight for a better way forward—through people power. We will only be as successful as the people pushing on the ground. Movements right now will either make or break system change. It will take people not being afraid to lose their privilege to speak truth. Because one of the biggest issues around this—and Eriel, you've spoken a lot about this—is that when people's privilege is threatened, they will do whatever they need to do to fight back. So, I welcome change. I welcome courageous voices. I welcome radical movements of social justice and equality. And I think we have to push like never before.

Conclusion

Phillip Dwight Morgan

In the summer of 2016, I was frustrated. On July 3 of that year, Black Lives Matter Toronto (BLM-TO) halted the city's annual Pride parade in order to shed light on anti-Black racism, just weeks after a shooter murdered forty-nine people in an Orlando, Florida nightclub. In the middle of the street, using a megaphone, members of BLM-TO enumerated the many ways that Black people in Toronto and, most specifically, Black people in LGBTQ2S+ communities, have been harmed by anti-Black racism.

The ensuing whitelash was fierce. Many Torontonians declared that BLM-TO had gone too far and had tarnished the mood and spirit of Pride. In the media, several outlets called BLM-TO "bullies." The story spread nationally and, with it, the anger, vitriol, and racism.

As a Black man watching the story unfold, I was shocked by the coverage of the demonstration, which largely revolved around whether BLM-TO's actions were appropriate. I saw no real discussion or analysis—at least not in the mainstream media—of the injustices that had spurred their action. The reporting not only felt lazy and uncritical but also propagated stereotypes and misinformation.

Exasperated, I journaled about what happened.

Afterward, I went online and was immediately confronted with viral video footage of the police killing of Alton Sterling, a Black man in the United States. I decided that between what was happening in Toronto and what was happening to the south, it was my time to speak up. Rabble was at the front of my mind as I contemplated where to submit an op-ed with my thoughts.

I distinctly remember learning about rabble. It was 2004, and I was in my third year at Trent University. September 11 and the subsequent war in Iraq had drawn people to the site because of the alternative perspective and coverage it offered. A first-year, Brennan McConnell, was debating American foreign policy in the dining hall of our college with great conviction. When I later asked him where he got all of his information and how he knew so much, I learned that he consumed a steady diet of Chomsky, Democracy Now!, and rabble.

Years later, in the summer of 2016, I must have known on some level that rabble would take my perspective seriously and not be afraid to publish a piece about racism in Canadian media at a time when most other outlets were content to amplify the BLM-TO pile-on. I sent the piece to Michael Stewart, then rabble's opinions editor (and the author of an essay in this book). With Michael's support, my reflections became the op-ed "Dear Canadian Media: Your Racism Is Showing." I wrote:

> Whether the issue is the niqab, fat-shaming, or the myriad other issues affecting marginalized groups, the CBC and other news outlets routinely tokenize guests, asking them to speak on behalf of an entire community and make a case for the discrimination they face. More commonly, marginalized people are absent from the conversation and left to listen to people outside of the community make prescriptions about change and reform. This is perhaps most apparent in the recent news coverage of the Black Lives Matter protest at Toronto's Pride.

I then went on to say the following:

> Given the abundance of information on oppression, intersectionality, gender nonconformity, Indigenous rights and the Black Lives Matter

movement, one must question why marginalized peoples are asked time and time again to defend the existence of their realities. At best, Canadian news media are blissfully unaware that oppression exists. At worst, they are actively trying to erase – not eradicate – oppression from the national narrative. I'll leave it up to you to decide.

Many of the words that I wrote back in July 2016 remain just as true now. Today's newsrooms remain largely estranged from social movements and the communities that birth them. Their coverage is disembodied —literally, removed from the communities and social relationships that provide structure to and animate our lives. The result is that reporting about railroad blockades to prevent the expansion of a pipeline into unceded Indigenous territory, for example, becomes a story about the inconvenience of the blockades to daily commuters. The blockades *were* inconvenient for commuters; the protest *did* travel across King Street *before* turning on John Street. This coverage is, in the most litigious sense of the word, objective—it is an accounting of facts. It is not, however, guided by a commitment to truth-telling, which would require centring certain voices. It does not acknowledge that access to power underpins the determination of facts and that being "known to police" reveals far more about discrimination in policing than the so-called "threat level" of the suspect.

As I write, in the spring of 2020, the first six months of this year have already left an indelible impact on the world as we know it. Like so many others, I have spent most of the year sheltering in place, trying to avoid contracting a virus that has spawned a global pandemic, anxiously following the news for the latest updates. Medical scientists still have much to learn about this novel coronavirus; at the time of writing, a vaccine has not yet been formulated.

But as a writer who focuses on issues of injustice, one thing is clear to me: *this virus is predatory.* Viruses, by their very nature, are tasked with finding ways of entering and then replicating themselves within a host, and it appears that Sars-COV-2 is particularly effective at exploiting the vulnerabilities of those it infects. Its symptomatology varies so greatly—ranging from difficulty breathing and fever to swollen joints, burning skin, and pneumonia—that it initially stymied the efforts of many of the world's best doctors and scientists to control its spread and impact.

The virus has wreaked havoc not only on individuals, by attacking their vital organs, but also on entire systems, by breaking supply chains, overwhelming hospital systems, and decimating national economies the world over. People of colour, the elderly, migrant workers, and incarcerated people are some of the most impacted groups around the world.

In Ontario, where I live, privately run long-term care homes have been deadly hotspots. But the disease's rapid spread in these facilities has as much to do with precarity as virology. Low wages and limited hours have forced workers in these facilities to take on shifts at other facilities just to make ends meet, and, in the process, spread the virus. Coronavirus is also spreading rapidly in Canada's prisons and jails. Migrant workers are keeping our food supply chains stable, but these workers are cut out of Canada's social safety net and have few protections from workplace exploitation and abuse, meaning few protections against the virus. The coronavirus appears to have infected and killed a disproportionate number of people of colour in Canada—though our government's "colourblind" tracking and statistical breakdowns will make it impossible to fully quantify its racial dimensions.

But this pandemic isn't the only major news story forcing people in Canada to reckon with systemic inequities. In May 2020, video footage of the violent police killing of George Floyd in Minneapolis sparked protests around the world. Protests in Canada have driven home the reality that despite our best efforts to feign exceptionalism, police brutality and anti-Black racism are serious problems here, too. Like a paper map folded unto itself repeatedly, the pandemic has put so much pressure on existing divisions that it has begun to tear at the fabric of society.

Mainstream media appears particularly ill-equipped to read the map for these connections, and I suspect that their failure is equally ideological and technological. I once read in a journalism manual that novelty is the basis for newsworthiness—the news is what is new. The manual then went on to note that the headline "Dog bites man" is not newsworthy—we live in a world where a dog biting a man is the kind of thing that we expect happens on a daily basis. "Man bites dog," however, could end up on the six o'clock news—such a story would be unexpected, unusual, and compelling.

While I love this simple and instructive example, I have often wondered what implications it carries for our news coverage of systemic oppression. In a settler-colonial society that routinely normalizes state violence, environmental degradation, austerity, and myriad other forms of oppression, have boil-water advisories in reserve communities and police murders become our "dog bites man?" Stories of systemic oppression happen every day. Does that mean they're not news?

Our news coverage seems to suggest as much. Longstanding struggles are often ignored or, if they are too big to ignore, covered as though they have emerged from somewhere new. In the search for a new angle or novel approach to covering a decades-old story, entrenched social problems are torn apart, removed from their context, and reconstituted as new, as "man bites dog." Police killings become the result of "a few bad apples," discrimination in our public education systems becomes an isolated incident at one school, and so on. This abandonment of historical context in the name of newsworthiness has devastating implications for the coverage we read. Egregious claims—such as the RCMP's repeated insistence that the institution is not a racist one—go unchecked. Expectations about novelty and newsworthiness prevent the fourth estate from fulfilling what was once seen as journalism's most valuable function: to provide a critical check on state power.

But for many activists, the connections between the systems of oppression and their impacts on individual people are obvious. This is because we live in communities whose members bear witness to the impacts of these systems. Whether the discussion is about how late-stage capitalism impacts workers, how the prison-industrial complex harms communities of colour, or how climate breakdown shapes the lives of climate refugees, understanding these relationships is a necessary and foundational component of our analysis. It is cultivated through our experience.

Journalism has been largely opposed to these insider-outsider distinctions on the grounds of very real concerns around objectivity, fairness, and accuracy in reporting. The *Canadian Press Stylebook*, a guide for Canadian journalists, implores reporters: "Everything that we do must be honest, unbiased and unflinchingly fair. We deal with the facts that are demonstrable, supported by sources that are reliable and responsible. We pursue with equal vigour all sides of a story."

The problem with this ideal is that it frequently does not translate in practice. Media concentration, combined with the decline of local papers and the staggering lack of diversity (ethnic, racial, ideological, and otherwise) in Canadian newsrooms, means that news coverage is often quite removed from the communities it claims to centre. Add to this that newsrooms do not exist in a vacuum and, as such, are not insulated from racism, sexism, transphobia, misogyny, and all other forms of discrimination, and one can quickly deduce why news so often misses the mark. Too often, media systems are complicit in perpetuating inequality and injustice. This occurs at all levels of media, from the stories that are chosen to how these stories are then reported and even laid out on the page.

The news coverage of the serial killer Bruce MacArthur drew criticism on many of these fronts. In a case that belied years of police neglect wherein the Toronto Police Service ignored warnings from Toronto's LGBTQ2S+ community of a suspected serial killer, reporters zeroed in on the gory details of the murders and the disbelief felt by many who knew the accused. A picture of MacArthur smiling in front of Niagara Falls became one of the most prominent images associated with the story after his arrest, making multiple rounds in the news cycle. This image—of an accused serial killer posing at a tourist destination—contrasted sharply with the Canadian media's tendency to use mugshots when reporting on racialized people accused of crimes, regardless of the severity of their offence.

White editorial boards and publishers beholden to the bottom line assign stories to white journalists with contact lists of key informants from a given community or demographic. Or perhaps an intern is tasked with monitoring local Twitter trends and finding a suitable guest whenever a topic trends or goes viral. Either way, Canadian media rarely cultivates reporters with the context and lived experience to report accurately, fairly, and truthfully on stories of oppression and activist struggle.

My own experience with rabble demonstrates that independent media outlets have historically taken the stories and viewpoints of activists more seriously, which is why the stories in this book feature reporting by people on the ground and invested in the social movements they write about. But independent media in Canada is under pressure in a very real way. Problems old and new threaten its viability. The issue of media concentration dates back to at least the early 1980s when, in 1981, Tom Kent authored the Royal Commission on Newspapers, which clearly identified the problem: "In a country [Canada] that has allowed so many newspapers to be owned by a few conglomerates, freedom of the press means, in itself, only that enormous influence without responsibility is conferred on a handful of people."

The other piece of this story is the loss of advertising revenue. Platforms like Facebook and YouTube have cut into newspapers' bottom lines and led to the shuttering of several papers, particularly local ones. By decreasing the number and variety of outlets, consolidation threatens media democracy, the concept that citizens have the right to participate and see themselves represented in the media they consume. Important local stories have been sacrificed as media conglomerates focus on larger markets. Investigative reporting budgets have been slashed, if not altogether terminated. In places where newspapers remain, they appear virtual carbon copies of one another, and a growing reliance on the news wire has reduced local reporting to a meagre column—"insert local story here." This is how Peterborough, Kenora, Windsor, and Kingston become virtually indistinguishable from one another and from Toronto, despite their different populations and distinct geographies and histories.

Creating and sustaining activist-fuelled media is difficult work, and it is not without its bumps along the road. On occasion, rabble has missed the mark in its work and harmed particular communities. Further, as one of the only racialized members of the rabble board, it is not lost on me that the organization has serious work to do. Nevertheless, I do believe the site plays a vital role in the Canadian media landscape, and that role is only growing in importance. What do activist media need to be better, and how can we help them get there?

The present moment holds many clues.

For starters, I believe that **hyperlocal is the scale of the future.**

The problems of representation, funding, and depth of analysis all coalesce around the question of scale. What is the scale of news coverage that we need in Canada?

Given the ways in which equity-seeking groups have been and remain historically underserved by the media, hyperlocal news coverage is necessary to restore some semblance of media democracy. The exclusion of the voices, experiences, and perspectives of oppressed peoples in Canadian media perpetuates white supremacy and invests in the well-worn narrative that problems of homophobia, transphobia, racism, anti-Indigeneity, and all other forms of oppression simply don't exist here.

Independent journalism can play a leading role in modelling best practices, and this must begin with reporting from and about these communities. Like any sort of community-based researcher, journalists and media outlets must take great care to avoid theft and exploitation. Specifically, I am referring to the hurt sometimes endured by communities when they freely give their time and energy to reporters, only to have a story published that does not represent that community's truth, let alone provide a benefit. This is often the result when a journalist imposes their assumptions and understanding on the story, effectively taking it from the community, rather than interview, document, or clarify an event.

Such instances of examples of theft harm media democracy by arousing suspicion and distrust of the media. Again, here, I draw on my experience as a member of Toronto's complex and intersecting Black communities. Indeed, there are many members of the community—including many talented journalists—who refused to engage with certain outlets simply because of the ways that those outlets have stolen from our community.

I have experienced this kind of theft first hand. In 2017, I was writing a story for a mainstream media outlet about discrimination in the Greater Toronto Area's education systems. My editor sent back comments that profoundly altered the premise of my piece, reframing my story about a longstanding history of discrimination as a story about one "bad apple" teacher who "should've known better." When I pushed back against the edit, the story's publication was delayed for nearly a month. As the editor and I went back and forth about the piece, negotiating which lines would remain and which ones would be removed, I found myself frustrated by the extra work that I had to put into justifying and explaining systemic racism to someone outside of my community who quite clearly had not put in the time or effort to understand the story or my work. That editor is well known among Black writers in Toronto: I've heard at least two other writers say that they refuse to write for her. This withholding is both a response to theft—the theft of our words, our labour, our insights and expertise—and a form of theft itself, insofar as it quite literally robs the public of the critical perspectives necessary to understand our world and navigate a better future. Across this country and across a wide range of issues, many gatekeeping editors are guilty of constraining public discourse as a result of laziness, or, worse, to avoid disturbing some of the most privileged among us.

It's no secret that Canadian newsrooms are overwhelmingly white. Despite its history of centring activist voices, rabble is no exception to this rule. The lack of ethnic and racial representation in newsrooms means that people from communities affected by some of the most pressing social issues of our time are not at the table for ideas meetings or editorial discussions—let alone actually publishing stories. At the CBC, Canada's national broadcaster, 90 to 93 percent of employees are white, according to a *Canadaland* report from 2016. Several contributors, myself included, have found themselves pushed to the margins of most major outlets in this country. Rather than rely on our expertise and insights, our ideas are forced into an editorial team's narrative, and contributors of colour are asked to debate the existence of racism, cultural appropriation, and other forms of oppression rather than speak to the concrete ways that communities have been impacted.

In an era of intense media consolidation and decaying local coverage, even the term "community" has become an abstraction, a mere trope used to imply a certain set of social relationships, but removed from the faces and lives of the people that constitute its very nature.

I believe that independent media can play a vital role in resisting the narratives and agendas imposed by the state and, instead, highlight the often overlooked priorities and needs of communities.

Secondly, we need **justice in reporting.**

The existence of oppression in Canada is a known fact. It should not be a topic of debate. Yet, year after year, versions of these debates find their way to the national stage. This brand of flagrant and gratuitous bothsideism impedes media literacy and democracy. The dogged pursuit of objectivity, fairness, and accuracy in reporting has led to an almost cartoonish commitment to amplifying "both sides" of a "debate." The problems with bothsidesism are well known as they relate to climate change, for example. Given that science is unanimous that we must urgently respond to the climate crisis, presenting both sides—the 99 percent of scientists who believe in climate change and the 1 percent who don't—actually skews the narrative. When reports give equal weight to multiple sides of an argument, devoid of context, the implication is that all sides are equally valid. The distortion has impacted the way in which this country talks about Indigenous rights, anti-Black racism, and social justice more broadly.

It is not enough for news organizations to reach out to writers whenever environmental concerns become front-page news or when #BlackLivesMatter is trending on Twitter. The communities fighting these battles are not governed by the twenty-four-hour news cycle.

My own experience as a writer is also proof that independent media can play a vital role in platforming and breaking down barriers for **new voices.**

My first op-ed for rabble, borne out of a deep-seated frustration with mainstream coverage of anti-Black racism, was read across the country. It was, in my humble opinion, an important intervention at a time when the media narrative was uniformly oppressive. Through that experience, I went on to become a monthly contributing writer at rabble and write for many of this country's largest news outlets. While I am grateful for these experiences, I am also acutely aware of how many writers from various communities remain unable to break into an industry that continues to shrink and, in the process, consolidate its perspectives.

Where are the writers covering the accessibility beat? There are so many incredible differently-abled writers and activists whose insights are desperately needed in this country. Similarly, the lack of knowledge around Indigenous issues in this country is a travesty. In the Media and

Reconciliation section of the Truth and Reconciliation Commission Calls to Action, the commission calls for the federal government to "restore and increase funding to the CBC/Radio-Canada, to enable Canada's national public broadcaster to support reconciliation, and be properly reflective of the diverse cultures, languages, and perspectives of Aboriginal peoples." The commission also calls for "Canadian journalism programs and media schools to require education for all students on the history of Aboriginal peoples, including the history and legacy of residential schools, the United Nations Declaration on the Rights of Indigenous Peoples, treaties and Aboriginal rights, Indigenous law, and Aboriginal-Crown relations." With a hyperlocal focus, renewed investment in citizen journalism, and a genuine commitment to communities, independent media can invigorate a stale conversation with new voices.

Finally, independent media can help revive **on-the-ground reporting.** The protests that have recently swept the world calling for an end to police brutality were catalyzed by the viral footage of the police murder of George Floyd. Floyd's murder has inspired murals and calls to action around the world, but it is the way in which his death recalls local circumstances that has compelled people to leave their homes and take to the streets. Here, in Toronto, Floyd's name was evoked alongside calls for justice for Regis Korchinski-Paquet and D'Andre Campbell. Over the past decade, the ubiquity of cell phones and access to social networking platforms have allowed people to tell these stories—stories that are often underreported or misreported by the mainstream media.

Journalists have been deeply immersed in social media platforms since the mid-aughts. This is partially because Twitter moves much faster than traditional reporting allows. Often, cellphone footage of an incident appears online before reporters have even gotten wind that something newsworthy has taken place. As with the viral footage of Floyd's murder, these platforms have proved useful to activists and storytellers alike. The problem, however, is that tweets and footage do not go through any sort of meaningful vetting process. Increasingly journalists report *on* instead of *from* social media platforms—the news cycle has now been further truncated to the lifetime of a hashtag. Without clear editorial processes, misinformation can proliferate with unprecedented speed and often with no onus or obligation to issue a correction when necessary. Simply put, Twitter is where news breaks.

When combined with training and preexisting community relationships, however, independent media has the ability to leverage the fact that many people now carry a camera and computer in their pockets. Independent media platforms could experiment with the amplification of diffused or networked storytelling—and independent media is in a particularly strong position to innovate while taking great care to consult and communicate with communities. While fly-over snapshots of communities have their place, there are some stories that can only be told on the ground, at a granular level, through trusted relationships. Imagine impact statements shared by communities along the entire length of a proposed pipeline or oil spill. Imagine coverage of a massive protest broadcast from inside the demonstration and from a variety of perspectives and positionalities. The potential here is great, particular against the backdrop of a cash-strapped media industry where investigative pieces are more and more scarce.

For too long, journalists have viewed themselves as scientists, treating people and communities as specimens to be observed at a safe empirical distance in order to preserve a too-narrow concept of "objectivity." But journalists are not scientists; they are people just like you and me, conditioned by their environment to bring their biases and assumptions to bear on their reporting. Without communities and thoughtful editors to promote accountability, framing that labels one emotional response "angry" and another "impassioned" go unchecked. To be clear, there is nothing objective about promoting hate, nothing fair about circulating a photo of a serial killer standing by a waterfall, nothing accurate about trivializing the loss of Black life with a sarcastic headline.

At its best, independent media has the ability to inform the public about important socio-political, cultural, and economic issues in a way that empowers people to make informed decisions and understand the world in which they live. At its worst, the media is propagandistic, constraining public imagination and circumscribing our possibilities. The end result is harm.

I find myself somewhere between these poles, seeking to learn so many of the vital skills of the field while carefully examining the ways in which violence has become embedded in so many of our practices. At the end of the day, I take comfort in knowing that I am committed to my practice and am part of a community that holds me accountable.

While there is much work to be done and many mistakes that are likely to be made, let us not forget that many of our breakthroughs arrive with faces.

Contributors

MATTHEW ADAMS For over thirty years, Matt has worked in nonprofits in a variety of capacities, including in education, communications, and business administration. He now works for a mission-based construction co-op. Matt worked at rabble in several different roles for about a decade and is a volunteer board member.

BARÂA ARAR is a writer and editor. She holds a Bachelor of Humanities from Carleton University and is currently an MA candidate at the University of Toronto, focusing her research on photography, gender, and colonial resistance. Her writing has appeared in *This Magazine*, CBC, and the *Globe and Mail.*

MARK BROWN is a board member of the Coalition of Black Trade Unionists and a member of the Canadian Union of Postal Workers (CUPW). In 2014, Mark was elected national director of the Toronto Region, becoming the first Black worker elected to CUPW's National Executive Board. He is currently the assistant secretary-treasurer of CUPW's Toronto Local.

DUNCAN CAMERON Born in Victoria BC, Duncan lives in Vancouver. A graduate of the University of Alberta and the University of Paris I, he taught political science at the University of Ottawa from 1975 until 2004. President Emeritus of rabble, he began his weekly column at rabble on April 21, 2004.

LYNN COADY is the author of six acclaimed works of fiction, including her novel *The Antagonist*, which was nominated for the Scotiabank Giller Prize in 2011, and her short story collection *Hellgoing*, which won the Giller in 2013. Her work has been published in Canada, the US, the UK, Germany, France, and Holland. Her latest novel, *Watching You Without Me*, was published in Canada in October 2019.

AMBER DEAN is an associate professor of gender studies and cultural studies at McMaster University in Hamilton, Ontario. She is the author of the award-winning book, *Remembering Vancouver's Disappeared Women: Settler Colonialism and the Difficult Work of Inheritance* (University of Toronto Press, 2015).

ERIEL TCHEKWIE DERANGER is a member of the Athabasca Chipewyan First Nation (Treaty 8) and a mother of two. She is the executive director of Indigenous Climate Action (ICA), an Indigenous-led climate justice organization. She is an active member of the UN Indigenous Peoples Forum on Climate Change. She sits on several boards, including Bioneers, It Takes Roots Leadership Council, Climate Justice Resiliency Fund Council of Advisors, and WWF Canada.

ERIN DESPARD is a landscape critic living on Musqueam land in Vancouver. Her background is in communication studies and human geography, and her work has appeared in numerous academic, artistic, and activist venues.

RUSSELL DIABO is a member of the Mohawk Nation at Kahnawake. He is the publisher and editor of the *First Nations Strategic Bulletin*. Over the past forty years, Russell has served as an advisor to numerous bands and organizations, including the Assembly of First Nations. He is currently an independent consultant.

MURRAY DOBBIN has been a social activist, freelance journalist, and author for over fifty years. He is a board member with Canadians for Tax Fairness and a past board member of the Canadian Centre for Policy Alternatives. He has written five books, including *The Myth of the Good Corporate Citizen*.

KIM ELLIOTT has had a life-long commitment to social justice and human rights advocacy that has been woven into her academic, consulting, and journalism career. She joined rabble as managing editor and has been rabble's publisher since 2006.

LEAH GAZAN is the current Member of Parliament for Winnipeg Centre. She is an educator by trade and has spent her life working for human rights on the local, national, and international stage. Gazan is a member of Wood Mountain Lakota Nation, located in Saskatchewan, Treaty 4 Territory.

ERIN GEORGE graduated from Ryerson University's School of Journalism in 2001 and spent two years working as a freelance journalist and photographer before being diagnosed with a disabling eye disease that prodded her to seek more stable employment in politics and communications. Her reporting sought to illustrate the scope of the movement by amplifying the voices calling for global justice.

SYED HUSSAN is executive director of the Migrant Workers Alliance for Change.

NORA LORETO is a writer and freelance journalist based in Quebec City. She is the author of *Take Back the Fight* (Fernwood 2020) and *From Demonized to Organized: Building the New Union Movement* (CCPA 2013). She writes regularly for many outlets and co-hosts the podcast *Sandy and Nora Talk Politics* with Sandy Hudson.

CHRISTOPHER MAJKA divides his time between research on the biodiversity and ecology of invertebrates, particularly beetles, a subject on which he has written over 150 scientific studies, and writing on climate change, ecology, the environment, natural resources, and political and electoral reform. He lives in Nova Scotia.

MONIA MAZIGH is an author, academic, and human rights activist. She has authored a memoir and three novels, and has contributed to several anthologies.

JESSE MCLAREN is a physician, activist, and blogger, who like Virchow, believes that if medicine is to accomplish its great task, it must intervene in political and social life. The movements he's been a part of and written about for rabble include antiwar, pro-choice, climate justice, refugee health, and decent work.

PHILLIP DWIGHT MORGAN is a first-generation Canadian writer of Jamaican heritage. His writings have appeared in the *Toronto Star*, *Maclean's*, *CBC News*, *HuffPost Canada*, and rabble, among others. He is also a member of Education Not Incarceration (ENI). In 2017, ENI successfully campaigned for the removal of the SRO program from Toronto District School Board schools. Phillip is a past board member of rabble.ca and was the organization's first Jack Layton Journalism for Change Fellowship recipient.

KARL NERENBERG is a journalist and filmmaker and has been rabble's parliamentary correspondent since 2011. Among his many awards are a Gemini and Best International Reportage from la Communauté des televisions francophones. In 2010–11, he wrote and co-directed *Never Come Back*, a feature documentary on the Roma people.

PAMELA PALMATER is a Mi'kmaw lawyer and member of the Eel River Bar First Nation in New Brunswick. She teaches Indigenous law, politics, and governance at Ryerson University and is the Ryerson Chair in Indigenous Governance.

BRENT PATTERSON is a political activist and writer. He has been a solidarity activist in Latin America and participated in numerous nonviolent movements. He is now the executive director of Peace Brigades International-Canada, an organization that supports the accompaniment of at-risk human rights defenders.

JUDY REBICK is one of Canada's best-known feminists and activists. She is the founding publisher of rabble. An author, her latest book is a memoir, *Heroes in My Head*. She is the former president of the National Action Committee on the Status of Women and was a spokesperson for the pro-choice campaign that won legal abortion in Canada in the 1980s.

SOPHIA REUSS worked as a part-time assistant editor at rabble from 2017 to 2020. She currently works as a labour communicator in the United States.

CORVIN RUSSELL is a writer, activist, and translator based in Toronto. He has been active in Indigenous solidarity and sovereignty work for almost two decades. Corvin is a past board member of rabble.ca.

EMILIE TERESA SMITH is an Argentine-born, Canadian-raised Anglican priest who has worked for thirty-five years with the people of Guatemala. Her work has focused on supporting Indigenous communities in Guatemala and throughout Abya Yala (Latin America) in the struggle to defend their lands and waters from predatory Canadian mining companies. Since 2012, Emilie has been the co-president of the historic Oscar Romero liberation theology network (SICSAL). She lives in Vancouver with her wife, the musician Patti Powell.

MICHAEL STEWART is a longtime writer for rabble and currently a faculty member in the English department at Camosun College in Victoria, BC. He started working for rabble in 2010 and is very proud of his time as the site's opinions editor from 2013 to 2017.

CARLOS A. TORRES is a Chilean-Canadian who writes on social movements in Latin America. An ex-political prisoner during the Pinochet dictatorship and a UNHCR refugee, he lived in Canada for thirty years when he worked for the Toronto and Americas Social Forum and the Socialist Project. He currently lives in Santiago, Chile.

CHRISTINA TURNER was an assistant editor at rabble from 2015 to 2020. She is currently completing her PhD in English at the University of Toronto.

REAKASH WALTERS is a writer, advocate, and lawyer. She is a descendant of Jamaican Maroons and the co-founder of Black Lives Matter Edmonton.

CARMELLE WOLFSON is a writer and social worker in Toronto (Tkaranto). She participated in an earth justice delegation to Grassy Narrows First Nation in 2006.

RACHEL ZELLARS is an attorney and assistant professor at Saint Mary's University. She is a co-founder of the Third Eye Collective.

ANTONIA ZERBISIAS spent eleven years as a CBC-TV journalist and then twenty-five years as a National Newspaper Award-winning columnist covering media, politics, and culture for the *Toronto Star*. She also hosted CBC Newsnet's *Inside Media* and, after retiring, became a columnist for Al Jazeera English.

MAHA ZIMMO is a Muslim womanist of Palestinian roots. She is a political analyst with an MA in international legal theory. Maha is the advice columnist at Chai Latte Diaries and a regular contributor to *sister-hood magazine*. Her poetry collection *rose-water syrup* was published in 2019.

Index